Contents

Library

This book is to be returned on or before the last date stamped below. Overdue charges will be incurred by the late return of books.

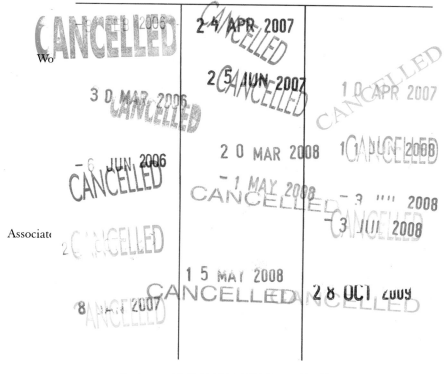

James Morris
Layout Artist, Emap Healthcare Ltd

Destine Simon
Projects/Production Manager, Emap Healthcare Open Learning

With thanks to Ed Tomlinson, International Marketing Controller, Smith & Nephew Wound Management Global Business Unit, and Jan Olson, Lecturer in Nursing and Midwifery, University of Wales College of Medicine, for additional specialist input.

emap healthcare

© Emap Healthcare Ltd 2000

First edition 2000.

Published by:
Emap Healthcare Ltd
Greater London House
Hampstead Road
London NW1 7EJ

Companies and representatives throughout the world.

ISBN 1-84244-034-9

Reprographics by:
Graphic Ideas Studios
Karen House
1–11 Baches Street
London N1 6DL
Tel: 020 7608 3639

Printed in Great Britain by:
Drogher Press
Unit 4 Airfield Way
Christchurch
Dorset BH23 3TB
Tel: 01202 499411

The Theory

1. History of wounds and the healing process

David Leaper

Interest in wounds is known to be almost as old as humanity itself. The history of wounds in the ancient world has been superbly explored by Guido Majno (1975). Some of the evidence is indirect; for example it is clear that early men were hunters, and cave paintings suggest that they sometimes sustained injury either on the hunt or warring between themselves (Figure 1.1).

In the early Neolithic period, it is known that the early hominids and australopithecrines inflicted wounds on each other during the hunt for food, or for self-preservation. Fossil records show that skulls were trephined, perhaps to let out evil spirits. The fact that there is evidence of healing shows that recipients of such wounds survived (Steinbeck, 1975) (Figure 1.2), and we can only assume that someone in these early societies had success in managing these wounds (and probably some failures). Perhaps there was an individual who built up experience and even some mystique in the practice — not unlike those in some undeveloped societies which still exist today.

Inflammation and infection

Some of the earliest written records containing a range of methods for healing wounds came from the Sumerians, who wrote on clay tablets (Figure 1.3), and the Egyptians, who used papyrus (Figure 1.4). These records show that the wound healer was a respected figure, but at risk of severe penalty should his treatment fail.

The Greeks and Romans also made accurate physiological observations and described many diseases. It is likely that wound therapies were mainly successful for minor injury; those injured in war or the gladiatorial arena were probably not so fortunate. The scourge of healing was infection; practitioners must have spent most of their time trying to prevent or treat it, and many materials and techniques were tried.

Galen (130–200AD), a Greek practitioner (Figure 1.5), worked with many traumatic wounds, and also tried to understand other diseases. His principal observation was that spreading infection in a wound usually resulted in overwhelming sepsis and death. However, when the body's response was rapid and adequate, the infection became localised. He described the formation of pus (suppuration) as

Figure 1.1 Early hunters' cave painting

3

Figure 1.2 Early trephined skulls show evidence of healing

Figure 1.3 Sumerian clay tablets — the first records of wound care

beneficial (*pus bonum et laudabile*); this misinterpretation resulted in practitioners for centuries following being taught that pus, and its discharge or release, heralded recovery. Wound healers would actively promote infection in wounds, using a wide variety of irritants including urine and faeces. It is likely that many patients who died of spreading infection had a wound that would have healed by primary or secondary intention had it been left alone. A few 'heretical' wound healers realised that wounds could be closed without the need to promote infection, but Galen's theory generally prevailed until the cause of infection became understood. This did not happen until bacteria could be seen; Pasteur (1822–95) showed that they were the cause of 'spoilt' wine and later that they were the cause of infections (Lister, 1867).

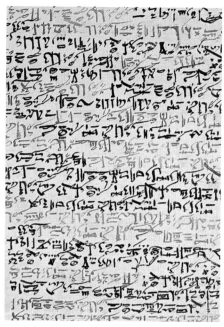

Figure 1.4 Egyptian papyrus

Galien natif de Pergame ville d'Asie, excellent Medeci viuoit du temps des Empereurs Antonin le Philosoph

Figure 1.5 The Greek physician Galen

Without the investigative tools we now use every day it is all the more remarkable that Celsus, a Roman (25BC–50AD), realised that inflammation was necessary for healing. He described the *calor* (heat), *rubor* (redness), *tumor* (swelling) and *dolor* (pain) of acute inflammation (Figure 1.6), to which has been added *functio laesa* (loss of function) — if the wounded part hurts we do not use it.

Over 200 years ago John Hunter (1728–93), the eminent surgeon, believed there was adhesive inflammation, which led to healing, and suppurative inflammation, which in turn led to infection. We now know these processes are similar, although suppurative inflammation represented infection; however, Hunter was correct in asserting that surgery would fail if inflammation with subsequent healing did not occur. Most wound healers advised that pus be drained, including Hippocrates (who described drainage of pleural empyema using a metal tube) and the Egyptians centuries before him.

Early wound closure

The primary closure of wounds was advocated in the Egyptian papyri and by many subsequent wound healers. However, there seems to have been a general reluctance to close wounds, as the risk of infection was high in shocked patients or when there was any contamination. Hippocrates resolved this by describing the use of delayed or secondary suture. He managed wounds at risk of infection by keeping them open, and irrigated wounds with wine or vinegar to clean them (Littre, 1839–61). When

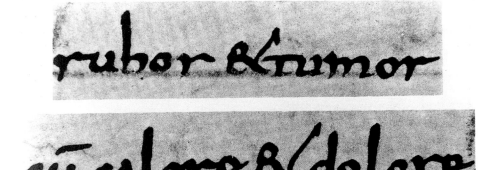

Figure 1.6 The writings of Celsus, describing the manifestation of acute inflammation

granulation (pink, vascular tissue which bleeds on contact) appeared and the wound was clean, Hippocrates recognised that closure was safe.

The Egyptians used sutures to close their mummies after evisceration and prior to embalming. The use of a thorn, with a thread of some kind attached to it, was also used to close wounds. They also favoured the use of adhesive strips to close wounds; these were probably made of linen with a resin or gum. Modern sutures are usually mounted on a metal needle without an 'eye' — the lack of a shoulder at the junction of needle and thread allows them to pass through tissues without causing trauma. The Greeks and Romans used eyed needles made of bronze, copper, and iron. These were not stainless, of course, and probably never sterile. Another clever device used to close wounds was the Roman fibula, on which a thorn or needle was passed between the opposing edges of a wound and pulled together by a thread rather like a cleat. Many fibres have been used as wound sutures (Goldenberg, 1959). Susruta, an Indian practitioner (c.380–450AD; trans. 1963), used cotton, silk, hemp and linen, whereas Celsus favoured the hair of a woman and Galen used a primitive type of catgut.

The formidable jaws of leaf-cutter and soldier ants were also used in wound closure, indeed it has been asserted that they may be used by some South American Indians (Wheeler, 1910). The mandibles are encouraged to close around a wound edge, the body of the ant is pinched off, and by the time the head and mandibles separate the wound is healed.

Unlike ants, sutures have prevailed in contemporary wound care practice, and natural absorbables (catgut) and non-absorbables (cotton, silk, linen) are now challenged by superior man-made materials such as polyglactin or polypropylene. Adhesive strips have also survived and the technique of using them to close opposing wound edges is associated with a low rate of infection and good cosmetic scars; they also avoid further trauma (useful in closing a fractious child's forehead laceration). Metal clips also produce good cosmetic wound closure.

Theodoric of Cervia (1210–98; trans. 1955–60) recognised in the late 15th century that primary wound healing could proceed without suppuration, and used bandages to hold wound edges together. He was, however, reluctant to suture wounds. Bandaging wounds can also support the injured tissues; in deep wounds this seems logical and many cultures of wound healers have advocated the use of bandages to oppose wound edges without suture. While this technique reduces the risk of infection in contaminated wounds, any excess pressure risks ischaemia at the wound edges or, more seriously, a compartment syndrome in deep wounds.

Haemostasis after injury or surgery

Most minor bleeding has been controlled by simply applying local pressure until clotting mechanisms are activated. Even arterial bleeding has been controlled by local pressure and the use of tourniquets, while the use of a ligature to tie a bleeding artery has been recognised for centuries. Previously, boiling oil had been poured into wounds to stop bleeding, although Ambroise Paré, the 16th-century French surgeon, substituted this for a far less traumatic treatment involving rose water, turpentine and egg. His patients were not in pain when this was used and many survived. Soldiers at Crécy were issued with cobwebs to help arrest bleeding, but where their original use as a haemostat came from remains obscure.

Wound cleansing and topical applications

Practitioners now use a range of techniques from 'clean hands' to full asepsis in managing wounds. Without today's knowledge of microbiology it is easy to realise how some of the more misguided techniques came to be used in the past. It is understandable that urine was used as a wound irrigant, particularly on the battlefield, because it is in plentiful supply and is usually sterile; however, it is less easy to comprehend the use of faeces. Metal oxide pastes have antiseptic properties, and milk and butter salves are astringent, but some agents may have a topical nutrient effect on the wound (such as sugar, honey, and amino acids). Personal hygiene, the simple act of hand-washing, prior to assisting delivery, was recognised in the 19th century by the Hungarian physician Ignaz Semmelweis (trans. 1941) to significantly reduce maternal mortality due to puerperal sepsis. Unfortunately, his contemporaries did not take Semmelweis' findings seriously; he lost his job and was ridiculed by the medical establishment.

Antiseptics are still used in wound management, but their toxicity must be appreciated. The use of phenol in antiseptic surgery was introduced in 1867 by Lister, but has now been replaced by aseptic technique. Antiseptics are efficiently used for hand-washing and skin preparation before surgery, although their benefit when used for pre-operative total body washing is less clear. The hypochlorites, disinfectants also used for cleaning toilets, baby feeding equipment, and working surfaces, were used effectively to debride wounds in the First World War; however, most practitioners have now rejected them for modern dressings, dilute antiseptics and techniques which are less traumatic and avoid potential toxicity.

Box 1.1 Landmarks in wound healing

10,000BC	Evidence of skull trephining
2500BC	Clay tablets in Mesopotamia — the first records of wound care
1600BC	Edwin Smith and Ebers Papyrus — detailed descriptions of Egyptian wound care
1267AD	Theodoric compiled a Chirurgia — proposed that promoting suppuration was contrary to nature and prolonged the healing process
1363	Guy de Chauliac published *Grande Chirugie* — discussion of open management for contaminated wounds (not fully understood until the experiences of World War I). Unfortunately, this reasserted Galen and the maxim 'pus bonum et laudabile'
1546	Giorolama Fracastoro's work *On Contagion* — first developed theory ascribing infection to invisible living entities
1600s	Compound microscope invented
1774	Von Scheele discovered chlorine
1800s	Julius Cohnheim showed that white cells (pus cells) migrated through capillaries into inflamed tissue
1800s	• Louis Pasteur established the germ theory of infection; showed that micro-organisms were responsible for fermentation; introduced heat sterilisation and the importance of asepsis
	• Robert Koch proved the germ theory by classifying bacteria
	• Elie Metchnikoff described the macrophage, phagocytosis and the production of antibodies
1811	Bernard Courtois discovered iodine
1847	Ignaz Semmelweis introduced hand disinfection to prevent puerperal fever on the labour wards
1867	Joseph Lister introduced the carbolic spray during surgery
1910	Alexis Carrel described the four stages of healing
1915	Introduction of the Edinburgh University solution of lime (EUSOL) as a wound antiseptic
1928	Alexander Fleming discovered that *Penicillium* mould released antibacterial substances
1940	Harold Florey and Ernst Chain developed penicillin to treat victims of the blitz. It was made available for civilian use in 1946
1955	Introduction of chlorhexidine as a wound antiseptic
1962	George Winter showed that wounds heal faster in a moist environment

Modern surgical procedures take place in sophisticated ventilated environments with completely sterile instruments. Wound management materials are often sterile and have strict controls on their manufacture and delivery systems. Antibiotics have little if any part in topical use (due to sensitivity and the emergence of resistant organisms), but are used systemically when wounds are clinically infected; the choice is often empirical, based on a knowledge of likely infecting organisms or on microbiological sampling, which is more specific but could delay treatment. In the early 1960s John Burke and his colleagues described the 'decisive period' when, after a wound is sustained, the tissues may be unable to mount a response quickly enough to be capable of resisting infection. During this four-hour period antibiotic prophylaxis, again given empirically, can reduce the risk of wound infection after contaminated or prosthetic surgery.

The wound healing process

The biology and biochemistry of wound healing in humans began to be more fully understood through the seminal works by Virchow (1860) and Metchnikoff (1905), giving modern researchers the basis on which to proceed. However, it is important to review how healing in humans evolved from earlier species. The more developed an organism is the more complicated this process is. Single-cell organisms, such as the Protozoa, are able to develop two separate new forms following division, while the amphibia can regenerate digits after amputation. Even some of the most complex animals, the mammals, can regenerate large amounts of tissue. In deer, for example, following annual shedding, new antlers can grow, involving epithelial and connective tissue components derived from totipotential cells present over the skull. In humans, however, only epithelial cells can regenerate to cover an epithelial injury; any connective tissue injury beneath can only heal by repair, which involves the formation of scar tissue (predominantly collagen, the scar protein). A defect of the skin or mucosa can be completely restored by regenerated epithelium. However, an injury to nerve tissue such as the spinal cord, can only heal by scar repair; unfortunately, function after cord transection can never be restored. In liver cirrhosis the hepatocellular function may be restored, because the cells are of epithelial type, but there is gross distortion of the liver architecture due to excessive fibrotic scarring of the connective tissue elements.

Regeneration involves cellular division of the epithelium adjacent to an injury. Cell migration across the defect repair is a complex process in connective tissues which involves an acute inflammatory response and formation of fibrous scar tissue (cicatrisation) and wound contraction. There is a fine balance between the formation of new collagen and removal of old or damaged collagen. Too much scar tissue may cause a contracture (in skin after a burn for example) or a stenosis (in a bowel anastomosis); too little scar tissue may be weak, and lead to an anastomotic leak. Bones may remodel after injury and fracture healing, but in other tissues integrity and tensile strength are never fully restored.

It has been shown that injury to the fetus in some mammals is followed by scarless healing associated with no inflammatory response. If this could be mimicked in the post-delivery phase it could restore tissues to normal physiological function and anatomical integrity. Further research involving the cloning of messenger ribonucleic acid (mRNA), and the sequence of growth factors and other molecules involved in healing, may achieve this goal. There is, however, obvious benefit from the normal healing response, as it allows the rapid arrest of haemorrhage and provides early temporary cover of the wound by formation of fibrinous clot and a scab.

Normal physiology and anatomy of resting tissues

The skin

Skin is an organ of protection. It resists the invasion of micro-organisms, rations fluid gain or loss, regulates temperature, protects against injury from radiation and electricity, as well as providing immunological surveillance. It also contains a vasculature and sweat system uniquely adapted to the body's thermal regulatory demands and an extensive neuroreceptor network serving as a finely tuned array of complex transducers of environmental information. Resting tissues are comprised of epithelia and connective tissue of many specialised types. Epithelial cells lie on connective tissue and the basal cells act as a germinative layer with constant division to form cells which replace old or worn out cells. A similar but much slower turnover of connective tissue occurs; both cells and the extracellular supportive matrix are constantly renewed.

Normal epithelia

These provide a protective layer of cells and often have specialist functions. Some have a single-cell layer, such as the glandular epithelia of most of the gastrointestinal tract, whereas the skin is multilayered with keratinised superficial squamous cells which resist the normal wear and tear of daily life. Characteristically, there are tight junctions between the cells of resting epithelia which are also attached to a basement membrane that gives a firm bond to the underlying connective tissue, such as dermis.

Connective tissue

This is comprised of the cells of blood vessels, fibroblasts, macrophages and other migrating white blood cells. These cells lie within the extracellular matrix (ECM) which has three main components:

Collagen This protein forms much of the fibrous tissue and is often called the scar protein. It is rich in proline and lysine, amino acids which are often biochemically assayed in tissue as an indirect measure of collagen content. Over a dozen types of collagen have been identified, but all have a basic triple helix molecule. During maturation collagen molecules become cross-linked, giving tissue strength. There is a constant dynamic turnover of collagen synthesis and lysis controlled by the matrix metalloproteinases and their tissue inhibitors; the balance can be fine in healing tissues.

Proteoglycans These form the 'glue' of connective tissue which is formed of protein molecules bound to various glycosaminoglycans (GAGs — predominantly hyaluronic acid, heparin, keratin and chondroitin).

Elastin fibres These are present in much lower quantities than collagen, and give tissue elasticity.

Specific tissues Other tissues have the ability to respond to extra physiological need. For example, skeletal muscle responds to increased use by hypertrophy (where individual cells increase in size) and the remaining liver can respond after excisional surgery by hyperplasia (where there is an increase of individual cells through regeneration).

Acute inflammation

Healing was commonly described as taking place in distinct phases, but is a complex inter-related process. Acute inflammation is the early response to injury and involves several processes and cascades.

Response to injury depends on the form and severity of the trauma. In general, the greater the injury-induced volume of tissue loss and healing burden, the greater the amount of resources needed to close and repair the tissue defect. In addition to the volume of tissue loss, the type of trauma can affect the healing process.

Haemorrhage after injury is arrested through vasoconstriction and the coagulation cascades. Exposure of subendothelial collagen in blood vessels causes adhesion of platelets through imbalance of blood vessel intimal prostacyclin and platelet thromboxane$_{A2}$. Platelet aggregation is also associated with other agents, such as serotonin, fibronectin and other prostaglandins, as well as chemical messengers such as platelet-activating factor (PAF) and platelet-derived growth factor (PDGF). In turn this stimulates the already activated formation of thrombin through the intrinsic and extrinsic cascades. The formation of clot (fibrin), together with platelet aggregation, seals the initial injury. Similar complex mechanisms control the fibrinolytic cascade through the balance of plasminogen activation and inhibitors.

Following injury there is a metabolic response mediated by neuroendocrine routes which chiefly involves corticosteroids (from the adrenal cortex), anti-diuretic hormone (from the posterior pituitary), aldosterone and adrenalin. The result is complex, but leads to a negative nitrogen balance from gluconeogenesis using protein. In feral animals this response is an obvious advantage in allowing them to respond appropriately to the immediate crisis. In hospitalised patients, however, the deleterious effects of protein breakdown and excessive or prolonged 'flight or fright' response cannot be safely counteracted. Appropriate pain relief, correction of shock and haemorrhage, with attention to nutrition, can modulate this metabolic response to trauma.

Shortly after the haemostatic mechanisms are activated there is an increased vascular permeability at the wound site with the release of serotonin, kinins and histamine. Chemoattractants such as PDGF and the cytokines and complement cause margination of white cells and their passage through blood vessel walls (diapedesis) through pathways which involve expression of intercellular adhesion molecules (selectins and integrins). Neutrophils are activated and release oxygen, free radicals (the hydroxyl ions, hydrogen peroxide, hypochlorous acid and myelo-peroxidase). Together with other enzymes derived from intracellular degranulation, these inactivate bacteria and promote their phagocytosis. There is an exudation of plasma components with white cell diapedesis. The chemotactic stimulus for white cells comes from bacteria, activated complement and transforming growth factor (TGF β) which further interact and cause the release of cytokines from macrophages and lymphocytes, particularly pro-inflammatory cytokines such as interleukins 1 and 6 (IL_1, IL_6). The chemoattractants and growth factors not only promote cell migration but also promote cellular proliferation of fibroblasts and damaged blood vessel endothelial cells.

Proliferative phase

Granulation tissue (fibroblasts, angiogenesis and macrophages) accumulates at the wound site prior to the formation of scar tissue. In conjunction with acute inflammation and granulation tissue, the monocytes and macrophages are involved with debridement of bacteria and damaged tissue together with regulation of damaged tissue repair. The control sequences are complex, but bacterial wall-derived lipopolysccharide (LPS) and lymphocytes promote production of enzymes known as proteases which can degrade collagen. This can be inhibited by steroids and non-steroidal anti-inflammatory drugs. Interleukin 1 (IL1) and tumour necrosis factor (TNF α), derived from macrophages, are responsible for many components of acute inflammation such as fever, activation of lymphocytes, and promotion of vasodilation, haemostasis and cellular adhesion. In turn lymphocytes fine-tune inflammation and repair by initiation, amplification and resolution through cytokines such as (TNF α) and IL_6, and growth factors such as PDGF and granulocyte- and macrophage colony-stimulating factors (CSF). T-lymphocytes also produce interferon.

Fibroblasts

Fibroblasts are normally in a quiescent state in connective tissue; however, after injury they are stimulated to proliferate, migrate and produce collagen, proteoglycans and elastin. Factors released from the clotting cascades and inflammatory process influence platelets, polymorphs, macrophages and lymphocytes. Growth factors such as TGF β, PDGF and epidermal growth factor (EGF) act as controllers of cell division, and inter-related actions regulate stimulation or inhibition of fibroblasts. There is an autocrine growth modulation through fibroblast production of interferon.

Fibroblasts also promote contraction of the wound; this may be more significant than epithelialisation from the wound edges in producing wound closure. The process of contraction has two main theories:
- That specialised fibroblasts, myofibroblasts, appear in the wound and secrete actin and myosin fibrils (similar to those in skeletal muscle). These fibrils can be seen on electron microscopy and (hypothetically) contract to pull the wound together

That fibroblasts migrate and cause a rearrangement of the ECM.

During the balance of connective tissue turnover after injury (particularly during collagen breakdown and synthesis) the tensile strength of the wounded tissue is at its lowest (the previously termed 'lag phase'). In the skin, a clot or scab fills open defects whilst wound contraction and epithelialisation occur. In some tissues, which may include skin, but certainly in the abdominal wall and anastomosis of blood vessels or bowel, wound integrity is required during the whole healing process, and this is when sutures are required. These may be made of an absorbable material, can be removed later or may have to remain intact indefinitely, as in an arterial bypass graft. Only 70–80% of pre-wounding strength is achieved in the skin when healed. Promoting fetal wound healing, where all tissue components regenerate without collagenous scar repair by elimination of acute inflammation, offers an attractive alternative. Repair without scar would have normal tensile strength and in skin would be cosmetically acceptable.

In some circumstances, such as prolonged inflammation, burns or infection, there can be an abnormal healing response. Skin contractures are unattractive and may cause functional disability after burns, and stenosis may follow infection after an anastomotic leak. Hypertrophic scars are red and thickened scars which stay within the confines of the wound. Keloid scars represent an abnormal connective tissue response where an over-abundance of collagen forms and spills beyond the confines of the scar. They are more common on the dorsum of the body and in dark-skinned people. Removal may exacerbate the disfigurement, but only partial responses can be expected from topical steroids, pressure or radiotherapy.

Angiogenesis

New vessel formation (angiogenesis) follows inflammation on the third or fourth day after wounding. As granulation tissue forms in an open wound this angiogenesis gives the red blush appearance. The new vessels are friable and may easily bleed following mild trauma. Once the wound has healed with maturation of collagen in the scar, the vessels regress and the red scar becomes white; in skin this can take several months.

After injury endothelial sprouts first appear from damaged vessels. These canalise and form loops, which are soon remodelled into arteries and veins. The establishment of blood flow brings oxygen and nutrients to the healing wound edge, while hypoxia at the wound centre is the stimulus for continued angiogenesis.

The migration and proliferation of endothelial cells takes place within hours of injury — a remarkably rapid response from their normally resting state. The drive for this activity comes from fibroblast growth factor (FGF), TGF α and β and TNF α which are derived from the cytokine cascades related to platelet aggregation and macrophage stimulation. As the ECM matures endothelial activity, initially related to clotting and fibrin formation, is followed by formation of hyaluronic acid and fibronectin, and later the ECM proteoglycans (where scar tissue turns from red to white).

Epithelialisation

Rapid restoration of epithelial surfaces after injury is clearly beneficial. This occurs principally through regeneration following rapid basal cell division and migration. Epithelial integrity is dependent on clotting, which is soon replaced by granulation tissue following acute inflammation. Re-epithelialisation begins with basal cell division adjacent to the wound edge or skin appendages, and there is some evidence that resting mesenchymal cells may be modified and become engaged in the process. Actual cell migration from the dividing basal cells is particularly rapid if the basal membrane zone (BMZ) is intact. Before migration the tight intercellular connections (adhesion molecules) are lost and a sheet of migrating cells forms. Finally the BMZ is restructured with collagen fibronectin and laminin and the epithelium is remodelled. The inflammatory response involving platelet and macrophage activation controls the response through FGF, EGF, PDGF, TGF α and β, growth factors and other cytokines such as IL1.

References

Celsus, A.C. (25BC-50AD) *De Medicina* (vols 1 and 2); Spencer, W.G. (transl.). Cambridge Ma: Harvard University Press.

Galen (130–200AD) *Opera Omnia* (20 vols). E.M., Kuhn, G. (eds). (1821–33) *Curavit* Lipsiae C Cnobloch.

Goldenberg, I.S. (1959) Suture and ligature materials. *Surgery* **46**: 908–1012.

Hunter, J. (1835) Lectures on the principles of surgery; chapters XII–XIV (notes taken 1786–87). *The Works of John Hunter FRS With Notes* (vol. 1). London: James Palmer Royal College of England.

Lister, J. (1867) Illustrations of the antiseptic treatment in surgery. *Lancet* **ii**: 668–669.

Littre, E. (1839-61) *Oeuvres Completes d' Hipprocrate* (10 vols). Paris: Ballievere.

Majno, G. (1975) *The Healing Hand: Man and wound in the ancient world.* Cambridge Ma: Harvard University Press.

Metchnikoff, E. (1905) *Immunity in Infective Diseases.* Binnie, F.G. (transl.). London: Cambridge University Press.

Semmelweis, I.F. (1941) The aetiologies, the concept and the prophylaxis of puerperal fever. In: Murphy, F.F. (transl.) *Medical Classics.* Huntington NY: Krieger.

Steinbeck, R.T. (1975) *Paleopathological Diagnosis and Interpretation: Bone disease in ancient human populations.* Springfield Il: CC Thomas.

Susruta, S. (1963) *An English Translation of the Susruta Samhita.* Bhishagratna, K.K. (ed.) (2nd edn). Varanasi: Chow Kamba Sanskrit Series Office.

Theodoric Bishop of Cervia (1210–1298) *The Surgery of Theodoric.* Campbell, E., Cotton, J. (transl. 1955–60); 2 vols. New York NY: Appleton Century Crofts.

Virchow, R.L.K. (1860) *Cellular Pathology as Based Upon Physiological and Pathological History.* Chance, F. (transl.). London: John Churchill.

Wheeler, W.M. (1910) *Ants: Their structure and behaviour.* New York NY: Columbia University Press.

2. Factors affecting wound healing

David Leaper and Keith Harding

No matter how skilled the local wound care or surgical technique employed, healing is likely to be impaired unless factors which adversely affect the healing process are recognised and treated.

Many systemic diseases have a theoretical basis for impairing the wound healing process, while lifestyle and local factors related to the wound site can also have an effect either singly or in combination (Box 2.1). The early identification and prompt treatment of such factors is an important aspect of patient care (Stotts and Wipke-Tevis, 1997), and should be a priority of management. Three categories of factors can delay healing: extrinsic, intrinsic systemic and intrinsic local.

Extrinsic factors

Drug therapy

Cytotoxic drugs These can have the most dramatic effects on wound healing, particularly vincristine. Whilst treating the malignancy, cytotoxic drugs interfere with cell proliferation, and can therefore severely impair healing. They can also cause neutropenia making the patient more susceptible to wound infection. The chronic nausea and vomiting associated with some forms of chemotherapy can lead to poor nutritional intake and impair digestion and absorption of nutrients.

Corticosteroid drugs These suppress fibroblast and collagen synthesis. Macrophages, essential to the healing process, are depleted by steroids (Morris and Malt, 1994). Treatment with supplementary vitamin A (retinoids) has been suggested for patients receiving long-term steroid therapy (Phillips et al., 1992). Steroids reduce inflammation by stabilising lysozymal membranes; Vitamin A counters this by destabilising lysozymal membranes, enabling the stimulation of the inflammation needed to initiate healing.

Non-steroidal anti-inflammatory drugs (NSAIDs) suppress the normal inflammatory response to injury and may affect healing by causing vasoconstriction.

Malnutrition

Malnutrition continues to be an issue for both patients cared for in hospital and elderly people living in the community. The problems of malnutrition in hospital have been reported since the 1970s in surgical patients both pre- and post-operatively (Hill et al., 1977), and more recent research (Dickerson, 1995) showed that patients continue to be at risk from protein energy malnutrition (PEM) following admission to hospital. Other studies have highlighted the problem of patients being admitted in

Box 2.1 Factors affecting wound healing

Extrinsic factors

Poor surgical technique

Haematoma formation is a common problem associated with poor surgical technique, and can lead to the presence of a dead space, encouraging infection as the haematoma is broken down

Poor wound care

Poor dressing technique or inappropriate use of dressings and wound preparations can impede healing

Malnutrition

Malnutrition can result in delayed healing and weak, poor quality scars

Fluid balance

Around 2,000–2,500ml of fluid are required daily for efficient metabolism

Smoking

In addition to its many adverse effects on general health, smoking has been shown to adversely affect postoperative scarring

Drug therapies

Drugs that interfere with cell proliferation, such as cytotoxic drugs, have a severe effect on wound healing. Corticosteroids suppress fibroblast and collagen synthesis when taken over a long period

Radiotherapy

Depending on the dose administered, wounds close to the treated area may fail to heal or heal slowly, while radiotherapy can also lead to weakness of the skin and other tissue

Intrinsic factors

Age

With advancing age the metabolic processes, including wound healing, slow down. Reduced collagen production and poor circulation can reduce tensile strength of healed wounds

Disease

A range of disease processes can adversely affect wound healing including:

- Anaemia
- Arteriosclerosis
- Cancer
- Cardiovascular disorders
- Diabetes
- Immune disorders
- Inflammatory diseases
- Jaundice, liver failure
- Rheumatoid arthritis
- Uraemia

Psychological factors

Stress and anxiety can affect the immune system, and can disturb sleep, which is important for healing and tissue repair. Altered body image due to disfiguring wounds or surgery can adversely affect patients' psychological state.

a malnourished state, with 50% continuing to lose weight in hospital (McWhirter and Pennington, 1994).

In evolutionary terms, we have retained the ability to maintain healing despite malnutrition. Healing has been demonstrated to take place despite poor nutritional intake, as 'biological priority' will put healing before less essential biological functions (Moore, 1959). However, from a clinical effectiveness point of view the prevention and treatment of malnutrition in patients with wounds should be a priority for both in-patients and out-patients as healthcare is an expensive resource. It has been suggested that improving the nutritional status of in-patients would reduce the incidence of complications and the length of hospital stay and potentially save the NHS £266 million annually (King's Fund, 1992). This is being addressed by:-

- Seeking an effective nutritional assessment tool (Sitton-Kent and Gilchrist, 1993)
- The use of the dietetic department as part of the team
- The use of percutaneous endoscopic gastrostomy (PEG) and jejunostomy feeding
- Enteral and parenteral support in intensive care and high dependency units early in the patient's admission.

Trace elements and vitamins

In addition to the problems related to malnutrition with protein, carbohydrate and fat intake, vitamins and trace element deficiency can also impair the healing process.

Iron Iron deficiency anaemia has been suggested to impair healing through a reduction in oxygen transportation (McLaren, 1992). Deficiency can also cause impaired activity of lysyl and prolylhydroxylases. Anaemia related to acute blood loss and shock results in delayed healing through poor perfusion.

Zinc Zinc is essential in fibroblast epithelialisation (Pinchcofsky-Devin, 1994). It is an essential cofactor for the enzymatic activity of 200 or more enzymes including protein synthesis (McLaren, 1992). Zinc is also involved in metalloproteinase (the chief enzymes for tissue turnover) production in the extracellular matrix. It is thought that zinc deficiency might interfere with wound healing by:

- Delaying cell division and proliferation
- Reducing the activity of inflammatory cells.

Zinc deficiency has been associated with the failure of wound healing in a number of experimental studies (Tarnow et al., 1992; Agren et al., 1991). It is unlikely that deficiency of a sufficient degree to delay healing is seen in normal practice.

Copper Copper is essential for the cross-linkage of collagen and collagen formation (Levenson and Demetriou, 1992). It plays an additional role in iron availability. The use of stored iron is inhibited in copper-deficient individuals. The patients most at risk of copper deficiency are those receiving parenteral nutrition (McLaren, 1992). Again, poor healing is rarely seen in clinical practice associated with copper deficiency.

Vitamin A More than 90% of vitamin A stores are held in the liver. Deficiency of vitamin A inhibits the keratinisation process and induces the skin to produce mucus.

This is associated with decreased collagenase production by keratinocytes.

Vitamin A has been used to counter the effects of long-term corticosteroid treatment (Pinchcofsky-Devin, 1994). It is an essential cofactor for enzymes involved in collagen cross-linkage and enhances the normal immune defence mechanisms, and so may be associated with resistance to infection.

Vitamin C Vitamin C is involved in collagen synthesis and a deficiency causes wound dehiscence, reduces tensile strength within the wound, and adversely affects angiogenesis. Defective collagen is produced in the absence of vitamin C, leading to weakened scar tissue, amongst other things. Vitamin C also boosts immunity by increasing cell numbers and complement synthesis. The use of supplements has been reported to improve healing rates (Mulder et al., 1998); however, while the results are promising their value is restricted by small sample sizes.

Poor local care

Poor surgical technique and wound care have been suggested to adversely affect the healing process (Bale and Jones, 1997; Morison et al., 1997). The inappropriate use of dressings, antiseptics and topical antibiotics, and the failure to identify abnormalities of healing, can impede wound healing.

Poor surgical technique can also impair healing in situations where:
- Tissues are traumatised by rough handling which causes haematoma formation
- Inadequate closure of the tissue layers leaves a dead space, particularly in association with devitalised tissue
- Diathermy or wound drains are used inappropriately
- Prolonged theatre time increases the risk of wound infection
- Sutures are not inserted at an optimal tension; too tightly causes tissue necrosis, too loosely leads to gaping and poor cosmetic results.

Radiotherapy

The use of radiation in the treatment of malignancy affects healing in a number of ways:
- There is a decrease in neovascularisation in the treated area
- Associated endarteritis obliterans causes small-vessel occlusion in the treated area
- Radiation of the abdomen and gut can cause mucositis, haemorrhage and fistula formation
- Radiation can adversely affect the absorption of nutrients and the digestive process.

Animal studies have shown that low-dose total body and local irradiation results in poor wound healing (Vegesna et al., 1993). Another study, in patients with soft tissue sarcomas, a delay of five days in starting radiotherapy dramatically reduced wound the incidence of problems (Ormsbt et al., 1989).

Smoking

Cigarette smoke contains a mixture of nicotine and carbon monoxide. Animal model studies have shown that nicotine inhibits epithelialisation, macrophage activity and wound contraction (Siana et al., 1992). Although no specific research has been undertaken on the effects of carbon monoxide on wound healing its detrimental effects on blood vessels and blood components have been well documented.

Intrinsic systemic

Age

In old age the inflammatory response, proliferation phase and maturation are diminished, indicating that the rate of wound repair declines with age (Mulder et al., 1998). Age mainly affects collagen synthesis; while it has been suggested that reduced collagen production weakens tensile wound strength, it may be more accurate to claim that the issue is the decreased elasticity of the skin (Lavker et al., 1986). Delayed healing in old age is reportedly due to the prolonged time taken to form collagen.

With the amount of collagen in the body decreasing by 1% a year, collagen becomes less soluble and able to swell, decreasing the breaking potential and predisposing the skin to the negative effects of trauma.

Additionally, with advanced age, there is a reduction in vascular integrity. The vascular walls become increasingly thin and the vesular cross-sectional area decreases by 35% (Gilchrist et al., 1982).

Diabetes mellitus

In the diabetic patient many factors are thought to impair wound healing, though no single factor alone is responsible (Kamel et al., 1996). A wide range of pathologies exist which affect healing including:

- Altered structure and junction of proteins
- Increased susceptibility to shear force damage due to collagen pathology
- Depressed host response with an increased risk of wound infection
- At a vascular level the basement membrane in the microcirculation is thickened, so reducing blood flow.

Hyperglycaemia also affects healing by:

- Making collagen more rigid and resistant to enzymatic digestion by collagenase
- Leading to osmotic diuresis and diminished perfusion and oxygenation related to dehydration
- Reducing leukocyte and macrophage activity then lowering fibroblast and collagen synthesis.

Poor diabetic control has also been shown to delay healing.

Diabetic neuropathy The precise mechanism behind the development of diabetic neuropathy is not fully understood but may be related to diminished blood supply to peripheral nerves. The sensory nerves alone may be affected or the sympathetic autonomic nervous system may be affected (dry, cracking skin) and motor nerves affecting small muscles (claw toes) may also be present. Neuropathy commonly occurs in the older patient with long-standing diabetes, and diabetic foot ulceration often occurs as a result of trauma to the feet, through the inability to feel pain or discomfort.

Macrovascular disease Macrovascular disease is accelerated in diabetics. Platelet aggregation leads to subintimal plaques which subsequently calcify (Bell, 1994). Macrovascular disease in the diabetic tends to be more diffuse, involving some vessels more than others (Strandness, 1995). Beyond the popliteal pulse the distal arteries of the lower leg are affected. Occlusion or stenosis of the macrovasculature in the leg may lead to ischaemia and gangrene (Bell, 1994).

Microvascular disease Microvascular disease is suggested to be due to the metabolic profile of the diabetic patient rather than an isolated vascular disease (Bell, 1994). The microcirculation is crucial, following injury of the foot, in bringing oxygen and vital nutrients and in delivering inflammatory cells which release cytokines and growth factors; these in turn stimulate extracellular cell matrix production for wound healing.

Jaundice

Jaundice may be caused by either benign or malignant disease. Its presence in patients with malignancy increases the risk of postoperative abdominal dehiscence (Grande et al., 1990). It has been suggested that this is due to an association with low skin prolyl hydroxylase activity and thus low rates of collagen synthesis. However, controversy does exist; a multivariate analysis (Armstrong et al., 1984) relating to wound dehiscence and incisional hernia in a group of surgical patients with and without obstructive jaundice found that raised plasma bilirubin was not of independent significance for either event. Poor nutrition was highlighted as the probable cause along with low haemoglobin, low albumin and the malignancy all being present.

Obesity

There are discrepancies in the literature related to obesity and delayed wound healing. Mulder and colleagues (1998) report that while some studies confirm that obesity affects wound healing, others found no relationship between weight and wound problems. The technical problems associated with performing surgical procedures on the obese patient may be as important as physiological causes, if not more so.

Psychological issues

There is an increasing awareness of the importance of the relationship between psychological and physical health. It has been demonstrated that both stress and anxiety can affect the immune system (Maier and Laudenslager, 1985). Little research, however, has been undertaken evaluating the relationship between stress and health in patients with non-healing wounds (Olshansky, 1992). A small study has reported that patients with higher cortisol levels (used as an objective measurement of stress) developed pressure ulcers whereas patients with lower cortisol levels did not (Braden, 1990).

Intrinsic local

Blood supply Throughout all phases of the wound healing process an adequate blood supply is essential. The re-establishment of the microcirculation and angiogenesis is the basis for restoring structure and function to the wound site. Tissue with a poor blood supply lacks the ability to proceed through the normal healing process. This occurs at the wound sites of many patients with chronic wounds, and is commonly associated with vessel thickening, which occurs with normal ageing. It can be accelerated in patients with diabetes or those undergoing local radiotherapy. Some anatomical sites are relatively avascular (cartilage of the ear) or have poor collateral blood supply (the extremities) and so the interruption of the blood supply to wounds at these locations can severely impair normal healing.

Changes in oxygen tension Research on the role of oxygen in wound healing continues. Niinikowski (1970) has demonstrated experimentally that variations in oxygen tension alter the wound healing process at different stages. Hunt and Pai (1975) demonstrated that variations in oxygen tension could alter fibroblast proliferation and therefore collagen production. Oxygen also enhances the structural support required for capillary angiogenesis. A review of the literature related to tissue oxygen cites good experimental evidence to support the hypothesis that problem wounds are hypoxic. However, human studies show little, if any correlation with moderate anaemia and blood loss (Mulder et al., 1998).

References

Agren, M.S., Chvapil, M., Franzen, L. (1991) Enhancement of re-epithelialisation with topical zinc oxide in porcine partial-thickness wounds. *Journal of Surgical Research* **50**: 101–105.

Armstrong, C.P., Bates, G.J., Balderson, G. (1984) Wound healing in obstructive jaundice. *British Journal of Surgery* **71**: 267–270.

Bale, S., Jones, V. (1997) *Wound Care Nursing: A patient-centred approach.* London: Ballière Tindall.

Bell, P. (1994) Vascular disease: aetiology and presentation. In: Boulton, A.J.M., Connor, H., Cavanagh, P.R. (eds) *The Foot in Diabetes.* London: John Wiley.

Braden, B.J. (1990) The relationship between emotional stress and pressure sore formation among the elderly recently relocated to a nursing home. In: Funk, S.G., Tournquist, E.M., Champagne, M.T. et al. (eds) *Key Aspects of Recovery: Improving nutrition, rest and mobility.* New York NY: Springer Publishing.

Dickerson, J.W.T. (1995) The problem of hospital induced malnutrition. *Nursing Times* **91**: 4, 44–45.

Gilchrist, B.A., Stott, J.S., Soter, N.A. (1982) Chronological ageing alters the response to ultraviolet induced inflammation in human skin. *Journal of Investigative Dermatology*

79: 11–15.

Grande, L., Garcia-Valdecasias, J.C., Fuster, J. et al. (1990) Obstructive jaundice and wound healing. *British Journal of Surgery* **77**: 440–442.

Hill, G.L., Pickford, I., Young, G.A. et al. (1977) Malnutrition in surgical patients: An unrecognised problem. *Lancet* **1**: 689–692

Hunt, T.K., Pai, M.P. (1975) The effect of varying ambient oxygen tensions on wound metabolism and collagen synthesis. *Surgery, Gynaecology and Obstetrics* **135**: 561–567.

Kamel, K., Powell, R.J., Sumpio, B.E. (1996) The pathology of diabetes mellitus: Implications for surgeons. *Journal of American College of Surgeons* **183**: 3, 271–289.

King's Fund (1992) *A Positive Approach to Nutrition as Treatment.* London: King's Fund.

Lavker, R.M., Zheng, P., Dong, G. (1986) Morphology of aged skin. *Dermatologic Clinics* **4**: 379–389.

Levenson, S.M., Demetriou, A.A. (1992) Metabolic factors. In: Cohen, I.K., Diegelmann, R.F., Lindbland, W.J. (eds) *Wound Healing in Biochemical and Clinical Applications.* Philadelphia Pa: Saunders.

Maier, S.F., Laudenslager, M. (1985) Stress and health: Exploring the links. *Psychology Today* **19**: 8, 44–49.

McLaren, S.M.G. (1992) Nutrition and wound healing. *Journal of Wound Care* **1**: 3, 45–55.

McWhirter, J.P., Pennington, C. (1994) Incidence and recognition of malnutrition in hospital. *British Medical Journal* **308**: 945–948.

Moore, F.D. (1959) *Metabolic Care of the Surgical Patient.* Philadelphia Pa: Saunders.

Morison, M.J., Moffatt, C., Bridel-Nixen, J., Bale, S. (1997) *A Colour Guide to the Nursing Management of Chronic Wounds.* London: Mosby.

Morris, P.J., Malt, R.S. (1994) *Oxford Textbook of Surgery.* Oxford: Oxford University Press.

Mulder, G.D., Brazinsky, B.A., Harding, K.G., Agren, M.S. (1998) Factors influencing wound healing. In: Leaper, D.L., Harding, K.G. (eds) *Wounds: Biology and management.* Oxford: Oxford University Press.

Niinikowski, J. (1970) Effect of oxygen supply on wound healing and formation of experimental granulation tissue. *Acta Physiol Scand* **78**: (suppl.) 334, 1–72.

Olshansky, K. (1992) Psychological factors in recurrent pressure sores. *Plastic and Reconstructive Surgery* **90**: 5, 9030.

Ormsbt, M.V., Hilaris, B.S., Noris, D., Brennan, M.F. (1989) Wound complications of adjuvant radiation therapy in patients with soft tissue sarcomas. *Annals of Surgery* **210**: 93–99.

Phillips, J.D., Kim, C.S., Fonkalsrund, E.W. et al. (1992) Effects of corticosteroids and vitamin A on healing of intestinal anastomoses. *American Journal of Surgery* **163**: 1, 71–77.

Pinchcofsky-Devin, G. (1994) Nutritional wound healing. *Journal of Wound Care* **3**: 5, 231–234.

Siana, J.E., Frankild, B.S., Gottrup, F. (1992) The effect of smoking on tissue function. *Journal of Wound Care* **1**: 2, 37–46.

Sitton-Kent, L., Gilchrist, B. (1993) The intake of hospitalised pensioners with chronic wounds. *Journal of Advanced Nursing* **18**: 12, 1962–1967.

Stotts, N.A., Wipke-Tevis, D. (1997) Co-factors in impaired wound healing. In: Krasner, D., Kane. D. (eds) *Chronic Wound Care* (2nd edn). Wayne Tx: Health Management Publications.

Strandness, D.E. (1995) Atherosclerosis in diabetes. *Journal of Vascular Investigation* **1**: 1 50–54.

Tarnow, P., Agren, M.S., Jansson, J.O., Steenfos, H. (1992) Topical zinc oxide treatment increases the endoglusus gene expression of insulin-like growth factor (IGF-1) in granulation tissue from porcine wounds. *Scandinavian Journal of Plastic Reconstructive Surgery* **88**: 4, 255–259.

Vegesna, V., Withers, H.R., Holly, F.E., McBride, W.H. (1993) The effect of local and systemic irradiation on impairment of wound healing in mice. *Radiation Research* **135**: 431–433.

3. The problems of wound infection

David Leaper and Keith Harding

Infection may be defined as the invasion of living tissue by micro-organisms. We live peacefully with 1×10^{14} micro-organisms living within or on us (Williams, 1973). These micro-organisms may be non-pathogenic; commensals or residents (which survive without harming their host), and transients (which can be temporarily cultured) which come and go. However, many bacteria can become pathogenic and multiply and invade if conditions are favourable; normally several factors prevent this.

The number of micro-organisms and the degree of their pathogenicity determine the establishment of infection. Host defences normally resist all but the most pathogenic organisms, but are naturally depressed by systemic factors such as shock, immunosuppression and poor nutrition, and local factors such as ischaemia, trauma or implantation of foreign material.

Infection delays healing, and in hospital practice this is particularly important. Hospital-acquired (nosocomial) infections are associated with more virulent organisms and are a greater cause for concern (Casewell, 1992). Misuse or over-use of antibiotics leads to resistance to these agents and emergence of new bacterial strains which may be carried on and potentiated by, for example, extra chromosomal plasmid mediations (Mehtar, 1992).

Even highly pathogenic bacteria need to be in sufficient numbers (inoculum) to cause invasive infection. Bacteria which are found in a hospital environment (nosocomial acquisition) are often resistant to antimicrobials. This virulence is associated with organisms which emerge following prolonged and excessive antimicrobial use, particularly antibiotics. Some bacteria only become pathogenic to humans in the presence of a foreign body (opportunists, for example *Staphylococcus epidermidis*) or may become pathogenic or virulent in association with another organism (synergy, for example, an association exists between *Eschericolia coli* and *Bacteroides fragilis*).

There are several barriers to microbial invasion. The most obvious is an intact epithelium. Skin, for example, because of its stratified squamous epithelium, presents a tough, dry surface, which resists colonisation by most organisms. Other epithelia produce hostile secretions or mucus, or have specialised cilia on the surface cells which sweep bacteria away. The stomach remains sterile because it maintains a low pH and an acidic environment. Some epithelial secretions have antibacterial action through their lysosyme or immunoglobulin content. Once there is a breakdown in epithelial integrity other mechanisms that resist infection include:

Non-specific antimicrobial measures

These include good tissue perfusion. When patients are shocked a contaminated wound is more likely to become infected. Patients with arteriosclerosis (with major vessel narrowing) or diabetes (with microangiopathy) are also prone to infection. The gas gangrene organism, *Clostridium perfringens*, favours anaerobic conditions — particularly if the patient is also immunosuppressed, old, or in a poor nutritional state, or when foreign material is present in the wound.

A good blood supply, as well as supplying oxygen, can lead to an adequate inflammatory response, which also resists invasion by non-specific mechanisms. Damaged tissue releases lysosyme, serotonin and histamine. Polymorphonuclear neutrophils soon appear at the wound edge and, following their respiratory burst, release oxygen free radicals which are microbicidal (and may also be toxic to tissues). Complement and anaphylotoxins are also found in the wound edge and aid in immobilisation of bacteria. Monocytes and macrophages are also attracted to the wound edge and release cytokines. An adequate venous and lymph drainage system also assists in the clearance of micro-organisms from the wound. Capsulated organisms may overcome these non-specific responses.

Specific antimicrobial measures

Specific antimicrobial measures (cell-mediated hormonal responses) involve exposure of white blood cells which then form antibodies. Antimicrobial antigens stimulate lymphocytes to cause proliferation and maturation of T-lymphocytes. In turn, through cytokine release and recruitment of T-helper cells, cytotoxic (antimicrobial) T-cells appear, macrophages are activated to phagocytose micro-organisms and further promote the acute inflammatory response. Natural killer-cell lymphocytes become active and B-cell lymphocytes are stimulated to produce antibodies which agglutinate and clear bacteria, together with non-specific stimulation of the complement cascade.

Bacteria involved in wound infection

Wound infection always delays healing. Several micro-organisms are pathogenic to humans and once natural barriers are breached, can invade tissues.

Staphylococci

The most common cause of wound infection after clean surgery (see below), staphylococci are commensals in chronic skin wounds that can become invasive and cause tissue breakdown. They reside in the nose of many people, and can easily be spread by contact when hand-washing and hospital hygiene standards are not maintained. Methicillin-resistant *Staphylococcus aureus* (MRSA) is a particularly virulent organism which can cross-infect wounds in surgical wards following inadequate infection control measures. Epidemics are rare but dangerous — sporadic appearance of MRSA in wounds may serve as a marker of poor infection control in wound care practice. Staphylococci cause local tissue destruction and pus formation (suppuration) resulting in abscesses and pain, with the cardinal signs of inflammation in wounds. Pain in chronic ulcers may reflect infection by *Staphylococcus aureus*, and

(e.g. ultrasound, CT scanning, isotopic scanning) which also permit guided aspiration and avoid the need for surgery (Lucarotti et al., 1991). An abscess is a localised infection caused by specific organisms producing enzymes which destroy tissue. Occasionally they can spread, even systemic, infections but tend to track in tissue planes and to 'point' on a skin surface before discharge or surgical drainage.

References

Casewell, M. (1982) The role of multiple-resistant coliforms in hospital-acquired infection. In: Reeves, D.S., Geddes, A.M. (eds) *Recent Advances in Infection* (volume 2). Edinburgh: Churchill Livingstone.

Cooper, M., Billings, P., Turner, A., Leaper, D. (1987) Intagerative microbidegical sampling is unhelpful after prophylactic antibodies: Proceedings of the Mediterranean Congress of Chemotherapy. *Chemioterapia* **987**: 6 (suppl. 2), 563.

Cruse, P.J.E., Foord, R. (1980) The epidemiology of wound infection: A ten-year prospective study of 62,939 wounds. *Surgical Clinics of North America* **60**: 27–40.

Dillon, M., Postlethwait, R.W., Bowling, K.A. (1969) Operative wound cultures and wound infections: A study of 342 patients. *Annals of Surgery* **170**: 1029–1034.

Keighley, M.R.B., Burdon, D.W. (1979) *Antimicrobial Prophylaxis in Surgery.* Tunbridge Wells: Pitman Medical.

Krukowski, Z.H., Mathesen, N.A. (1988) Ten-year computerised audit of infection after general surgery. *British Journal of Surgery* **75**: 857–861.

Lucarotti, M.E., Virjee, J., Thomas, W.E.G., Leaper, D.I. (1991) Intra-abdominal abscesses. *Surgery* **1**: 2235–2341.

Raachave, D. (1992) Wound contamination and postoperative infection. In: Taylor, E.W. (ed.) *Infection in Surgical Practice.* Oxford: Oxford University Press.

Mehtar, S. (1992) Action of antibodies and the development of antibiotic resistance. In: Taylor, E.W. (ed.) *Infection in Surgical Practice.* Oxford: Oxford University Press.

Williams, R.E.O. (1973) Benefit and mischief from commensal bacterias. *Journal of Clinical Pathology* **26**: 811–818.

The Practice

4. Principles and practices of wound assessment and management

Sue Bale

Nurses undertaking wound assessments need to integrate such activities with their knowledge of the normal healing process and pathophysiologies. It is widely accepted that if patient outcomes are to be successful, assessment must be comprehensive, carefully documented and monitored using standard, well-defined criteria (Thomas et al., 1994). However, the dilemma for many nurses is which of the many wound assessment tools to use. There are different tools for surgically closed and open wounds (Morison, 1992); others run over several pages and are extremely detailed (Miller and Dyson, 1996). Teams of nurses may find it helpful to review the available tools and select the one most appropriate to both their needs and those of their patients.

Wound size and shape

For surgically-created wounds, size has a direct bearing on the expected healing time. Marks et al. (1983) measured a large number of abdominal, pilonidal and axillary wounds throughout the healing phase. Using these data they were able to predict, for each wound aetiology, when wounds of a given size should heal. Recent research by Margolis (1999) has shown than the rate of change of wound size over 4 weeks in patients with venous ulcers also indicates which ulcers are likely to heal or not.

Where undermining of the skin edge occurs, assessment and measurement is more difficult and less accurate, as all contours of the wound cannot be seen (Figure 4.1).

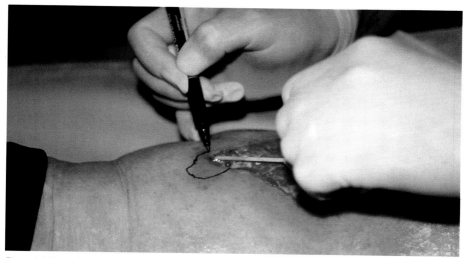

Figure 4.1 Measuring undermining of the skin

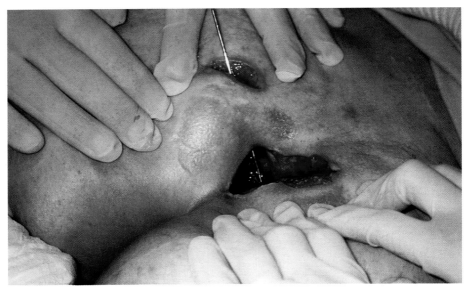

Figure 4.2 A deep sinus tract connecting two pressure ulcers

Chronic wounds are associated with irregular wound shape (Bale and Jones, 1997). Undermining tracts and sinuses impede wound drainage and are often associated with difficulty in dressing (Figure 4.2). For all wounds that result in a cavity the ideal shape is a 'boat', where the wound edges are easily kept apart and exudate can drain freely from the cavity (Figure 4.3).

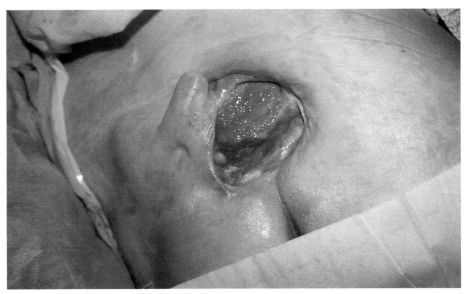

Figure 4.3 A boat-shaped pressure ulcer, allowing free drainage of exudate

Exudate

Wound exudate is a key characteristic in determining the choice of dressing material. Manufacturers' instructions recommend products for use on heavily, moderately or lightly exuding wounds. The dilemma for nurses, however, is how to define these terms. A rough guide to determining the level of exudate production is to look at the frequency of dressing change, and the dressing material being used. Wounds requiring daily or more frequent changes due to saturation of an appropriate modern dressing are heavily exuding (Figure 4.4). Moderate exudate equates to dressing changes every 1–3 days, and light exudate to dressing changes every 4–7 days.

Wound measurement

It is important to accurately measure a wound over time for the purposes of both documentation and evaluation of the treatment regimen. There are several methods of wound measurement using equipment of varying sophistication. Some do not lend themselves to routine use by nurses in clinical areas (Plassmann et al., 1994a). Ideally a measurement system should be precise and accurate, and easy to use without coming into contact with the wound itself (Melhuish et al., 1994).

Acetate tracing

The most common practice for assessing wound area is the use of acetate tracings (Majeske, 1992). Problems related to cleansing the acetate and the risk of cross-infection through direct contact with the wound have been solved by the development of a two-layer system with a disposable patient contact layer (Figure 4.5) (Melhuish et al., 1994).

Inaccuracies have been identified in this technique where nurses differ in their method of defining the wound edge and calculating the area thereafter (Plassman et al., 1994b). It should be recognised that there are opportunities for inaccuracies to occur when tracing the wound edge. Whilst recognising inaccuracy as being a problem, acetate tracings can be recommended over other types of measurement for routine use because it is rapid and inexpensive, requires minimal training and gives instant results.

Acetate tracings and photography can measure area but not volume and are only useful for flat or superficial wounds. In cavity wounds the measurement of depth of estimate volume is an important aspect of the assessment process.

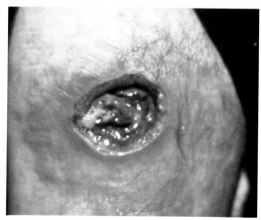
Figure 4.4 A heavily exuding pressure ulcer on the knee

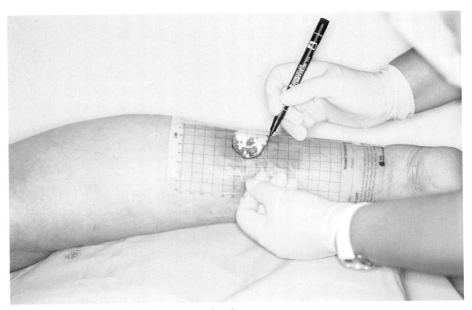

Figure 4.5 Using a two-layer system to measure a leg ulcer

Figure 4.6 Photographs can be extremely useful for recording the condition of the wound

Photographs and video images

Photographs are extremely useful for recording the condition of the wound and the surrounding skin over time (Figure 4.6). They provide a permanent record of the wound and should (ideally) have a label near the wound stating the patient's initials and the date the photograph was taken. This method is relatively cheap and easily available. For community and practice nurses Polaroid cameras are portable and quite robust.

It is, however, difficult to use photographs for the purposes of measurement using standard 35mm cameras or Polaroid, as it is difficult to standardise the camera angle. This can lead to a 10% margin of error, depending on the angle at which the camera is held (Plassmann et al., 1994a). More expensive, time-consuming and technically difficult, is

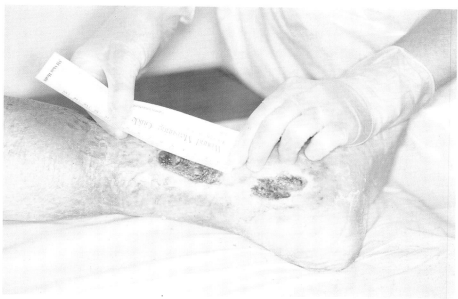

Figure 4.7 Using a disposable paper ruler to estimate maximum ulcer length

the use of stereo photogrammetry — stereo pairs of photographs which can give three-dimensional profiles of the wound (Melhuish, 1994). In addition, digital imaging is becoming more widely used. Images can be taken at the bedside using a digital camera and loaded onto a PC for storage, so that the wound's progress can be recorded visually.

Ruler and cotton bud

As with acetate tracing a ruler is an inexpensive, easily-available tool for recording how a wound is progressing over a period of time (Figure 4.7). A cotton bud can be used to measure the depth of the wound (Figure 4.8). There is inevitably a degree of variability between nurses, and for maximum value and accuracy all dimensions (length, breadth and depth) should ideally be recorded by the same nurse on each occasion (Bale and Jones, 1997).

Kundin Gauge

This is a disposable system which is placed into the cavity wound and acts as a three-dimensional ruler. The Kundin gauge cannot measure undermining and tracking, and has been reported to underestimate wound size where there are irregular contours (Plassmann et al., 1994b).

Wound moulding

The use of a dental impression material (Jeltrate) has been described for making casts of a cavity wound (Resch et al., 1988). Jeltrate powder is mixed with water to form a paste, which is spooned into the wound. It sets in about three minutes to form a permanent cast

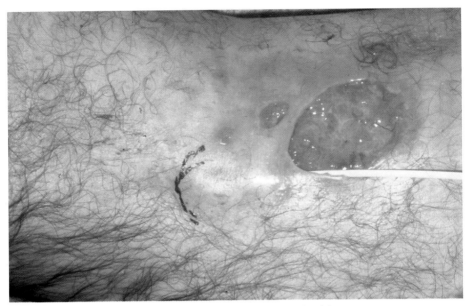

Figure 4.8 A cotton bud can be used to measure wound tracking and undermining

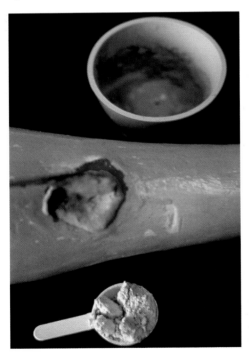

Figure 4.9 Using Jeltrate to make a cast of a model cavity wound

of the cavity wound (Figure 4.9). Volume can then be estimated by water displacement or by weighing. The authors describe its ease of use, but identify problems in using Jeltrate with deep wounds and where there is extensive undermining, where the material cannot fill the cavity.

Structured light

Parallel beams of light are shone at an angle onto the wound, and a camera is connected to an image processing computer which picks up the image (Figure 4.10). A three-dimensional representation of the wound is produced. The initial picture is taken in seconds, whilst measurement and calculation of wound volume takes under five minutes (Plassmann et al., 1994b). Although commercially available, this equipment is bulky, heavy to transport and expensive. The

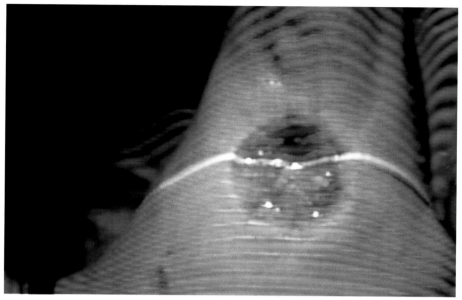

Figure 4.10 Beams of structured light bend when shone onto a cavity wound

system cannot measure what it cannot see, so cannot be used with undermining areas and deep wounds. However, structured light has been demonstrated to be an accurate method of assessing both wound volume and area and is potentially useful for research studies.

The literature suggests that, for nurses working in both hospital and community settings, the use of acetate sheets to measure area and a ruler and cotton bud to measure wound volume are the most practical. These measurements can be easily taken and documented in patients' records. Nurses working in specialist units, or undertaking research projects, may find the more time-consuming, expensive but more accurate systems more appropriate.

Documentation

The documentation of a wound and its re-evaluation throughout the healing process is essential to proper management and effective patient care (Hess, 1995). In addition to measuring wound dimensions other documented information might include:

- A classification of the wound aetiology, such as venous leg ulcer, mixed leg ulcer, Grade 2 pressure ulcer, neuropathic foot ulcer, surgical wound dehiscence
- The anatomical position of the wound; this may be described using words or codes, such as abdominal, gaiter, sacral (Thomas et al., 1994), or a pictorial outline of the body (Hess, 1995)
- Appearance of the wound bed, such as sloughy, granulating
- Appearance of the skin surrounding the wound, such as lipodermatosclerosis, erythema, maceration

- Exudate level
- Wound odour
- Wound pain
- Additional information which is pertinent to the wound aetiology, such as the ankle-brachial pressure index for leg ulceration, the chosen risk assessment score for pressure damage, the Wagner score for the severity of diabetic foot ulceration
- Dressing used and frequency of dressing change
- Other products and devices used in managing the wound, such as pressure-relieving bed or cushion, bandaging system, orthotic footwear.

Documentation of wound assessment and intervention may be incorporated into the patient's existing care plan (Bale and Jones, 1997), without the need for another proforma. It may be restricted to the basic information needed where it is impractical to routinely undertake more detailed documentation. However, centres involved in research have developed databases and presented the results of using comprehensive systems (Thomas et al., 1994).

Condition of the wound bed

The normal wound bed

Sutured/primary closure Erythema and induration are commonly associated with the inflammatory phase of healing in sutured wounds (Figure 4.11).

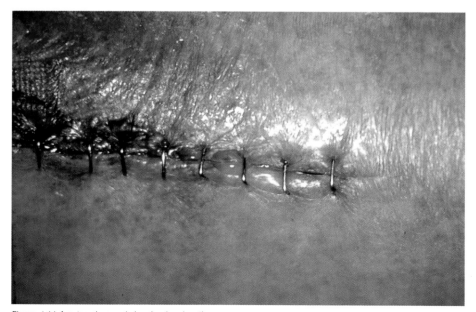

Figure 4.11 A sutured wound showing local erythema

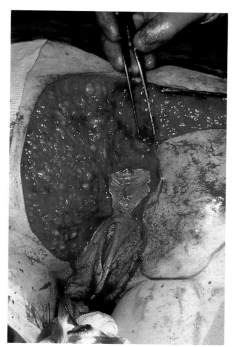

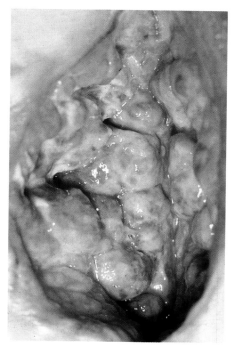

Figure 4.12 A freshly excised wound at the time of surgery

Figure 4.13 Pre-granulation tissue on an abdominal wound

Freshly excised At the time of surgery and in the days immediately following, granulation tissue has yet to appear (Figure 4.12). At this time the wound contains adipose tissue and/or muscle with occasionally small haematomas or diathermy marks (Figure 4.13).

Granulation tissue At around 10–14 days granulation tissue appears on the wound bed (Figure 4.14a). Healthy granulation tissue is red/pink/yellow in appearance and has a firm texture with a typical cobblestone appearance.

Wound contraction Where a large amount of tissue has been excised the process of wound contraction plays an important role in healing (Figure 4.14b). A mature scar which is 10% of the size of the original wound is a result of both wound contraction and granulation tissue formation. This does not necessarily result in any loss of normal functioning in the area, and the patient retains a full range of movement.

Epithelialisation/maturation Epithelial cells grow out from the wound edge and from undamaged hair follicles in the wound bed. Once these cells have expanded in area, wound closure is complete (Figure 4.15). However, the process of scar maturation takes place over a number of months and years.

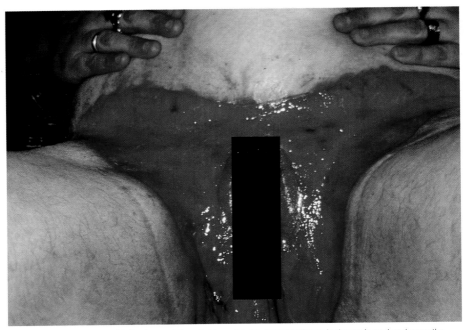

Figure 4.14a A large wound following excision of skin and subcutaneous tissue in the groin and perineum;the wound is covered with granulation tissue

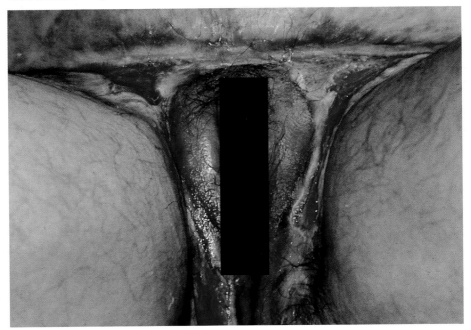

Figure 4.14b Six weeks later the wound has contracted

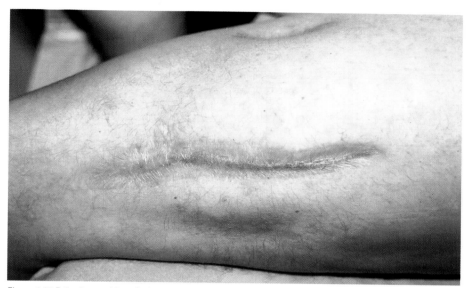

Figure 4.15 Following excision of a large abscess, this wound healed by secondary intention

The abnormal wound bed

Slough/necrosis When damage occurs and tissue is deprived of a blood supply, it dies. The dead, desiccated tissue forms slough on the wound bed (Figure 4.16). When exposed to the air necrotic epidermis quickly dries to form a hard leathery eschar (Figure 4.17) (Thomas et al., 1996).

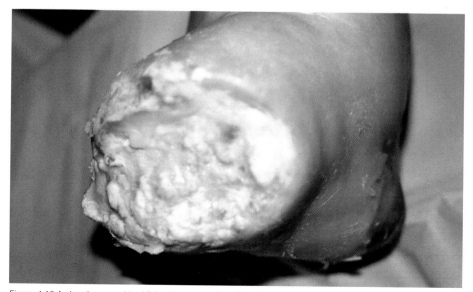

Figure 4.16 A sloughy wound bed following amputation of the forefoot due to gangrene of the toes

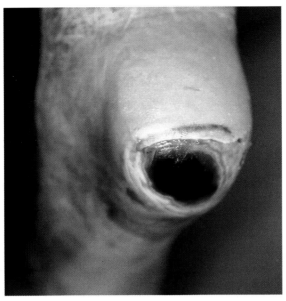

Figure 4.17 Necrotic eschar in a pressure ulcer of the heel

Where extensive tissue damage has occurred the necrosis may extend down to muscle and even bone. However, the texture of this devitalised tissue is often soft and yellow or grey in appearance (Dealey, 1994). The literature cites the presence of slough and/or necrosis on a wound bed as being a focus for infection that leads to impaired healing (Goode, 1995; Bergstrom et al., 1994). Although the physical properties of necrosis and slough are not well understood the characteristics of the different types of devitalised tissue have been described (Bale, 1997).

Infection   As distinct from sutured wounds, all open wounds will quickly become colonised by bacteria; for the most part these do not delay or prevent healing. When pathogenic organisms multiply and are found in large numbers in the wound, infection can occur. Assessing when a normally colonised wound becomes an infected wound is a difficult aspect of patient assessment. Patients with infected open wounds rarely become systemically unwell in the early stages, unlike those with infected sutured wounds. However, vigilance is needed throughout the healing phase, and nurses should be aware of the criteria which indicate the presence of infection:

- The wound remains the same size for a number of weeks or starts to grow
- The appearance of the wound bed changes from healthy (Figure 4.18) to unhealthy (Figure 4.19) and is characterised by flimsy, friable, red granulation tissue which bleeds readily on light contact
- The wound becomes malodorous (Figure 4.20)
- The exudate levels increase over a short period
- The presence of superficial bridging can be seen within the tissue
- A large number of pathogenic organisms is grown from the wound.

Chapter 3 discusses the issues related to wound infection. There is much debate about which techniques (swabs or biopsies) best diagnose infection, and also the number of bacteria required to confirm infection. To date there are no clear guidelines to direct nurses in their management of patients with potentially infected wounds. Cutting and Harding (1994) suggest that the clinical appearance of the wound bed indicates the presence of a wound infection. These clinical signs include:

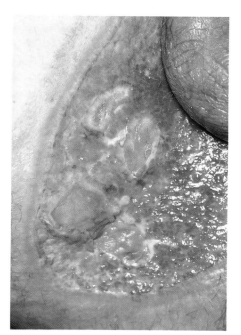

Figure 4.18 A healthy wound bed with granulation tissue and islands of epithelialisation

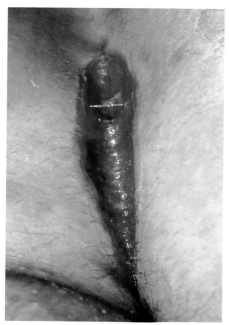

Figure 4.19 A pilonidal sinus excision wound showing clinical signs of infection

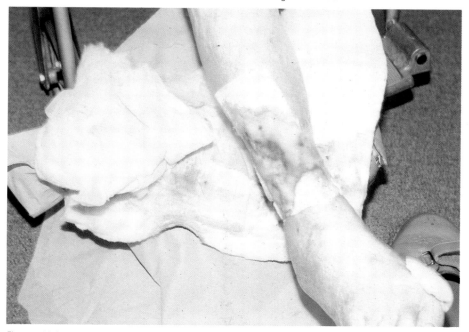

Figure 4.20 A wound with pseudomonas infection, producing malodorous exudate

- Flimsy, friable granulation tissue
- Unexpected pain or discomfort in the wound
- Discolouration of the tissue
- Pocketing at the base of the wound
- Bridging of the tissues
- A delay in healing.

To further support these clinical signs, other researchers (Stotts, 1995; Heggers, 1998) recommend the additional use of quantitative bacteriology as a reliable method of confirming the presence of infection. It should be recognised, however, that in many circumstances such techniques are not available or practicable.

Practical issues related to wound management

Flat wounds

The level of exudate production will influence the choice of dressing material. Wounds producing little or no exudate can become dry and desiccated and require a dressing which adds or retains moisture. Large flat wounds, especially those surgically created, such as skin graft donor sites, can be heavily exuding and require absorbent materials. Unless exudate is controlled and absorbed, both the wound and surrounding skin will become macerated, leading to pain and skin breakdown (Figure 4.21).

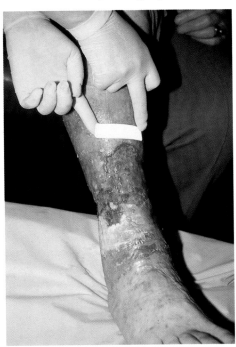

Securing dressings to some wound sites, such as the thigh and back, can be challenging. A combination of retention bandages and clothing can be used to avoid the skin being stripped by adhesive tapes (Morison et al., 1997). The current range of dressing materials is discussed in Chapter 5.

Cavity wounds

The products selected to manage cavity wounds should be appropriate to both the level of exudate and the wound shape. The aim is to keep the wound edges apart and prevent premature closure and dead spaces forming within the cavity. In acute wounds, whenever possible, the surgeon aims to create a cavity shape which allows free drainage of exudate. This may involve laying open all tracts and sinuses. Surgical intervention under general or local anaesthetic may be required for some patients with chronic wounds where

Figure 4.21 A heavily exuding leg ulcer with macerated skin

there are underlying tracts or sinuses, or where poor wound shape is preventing free drainage of exudate.

Wound debridement

There are several methods of wound debridement; the choice will depend on the nurse's ability and the range of treatments available.

Sharp debridement This involves the removal of sloughy tissue using a scalpel or scissors (Figure 4.22), continued until bleeding tissue is encountered or more conservatively by cutting off loose or hanging tissue. The technique may be undertaken at the patient's bedside in hospital, in the community or in an outpatient clinic. Where extensive devitalised tissue is present, a surgeon may wish to undertake surgical debridement in theatre.

There has been much debate on the nurse's role in undertaking sharp debridement; in the USA courses are available for training nurses but, apart from workshop sessions, no such training is available in the UK. Debridement of loose, devitalised tissue is relatively simple and easy to achieve using a scalpel or scissors. Extreme care must be taken, however, where the underlying structures include blood vessels, nerves or tendons (Bale, 1997). Sharp debridement may also be assisted by the use of an enzymatic or autolytic agent in the seven days preceding the procedure to soften and loosen the tissue to be removed.

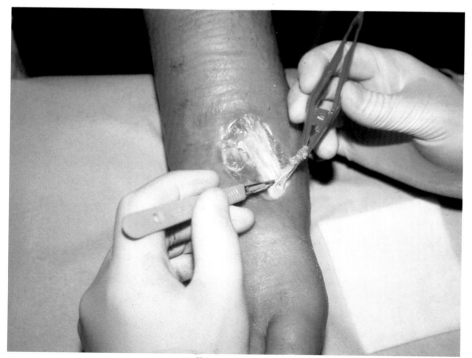

Figure 4.22 Sharp wound debridement

Enzymatic agents Awareness and use of new enzymatic agents in wound debridement is increasing. A variety of collagenases have been reported to be useful in achieving debridement (Jing, 1995; Glyantsev et al., 1997; Campbell et al., 1987), and plant enzymes are being developed, though at present there is limited evidence of their effectiveness (Martin et al., 1996).

Autolytic debridement Compared to more traditional therapies the use of moisture-donating dressings (such as hydrogels) have been demonstrated to be effective in facilitating debridement (Mulder, 1995). The autolytic process uses the body's own enzymes to break down devitalised tissue when maintained in a moist or wet environment.

Larval therapy In recent years there has been a resurgence in the use of larvae (maggots) to achieve wound debridement. The technique has been described in the literature (Thomas et al., 1996; Church, 1996), though randomised controlled trials comparing larval therapy with other enzymatic therapies are as yet unavailable.

The choice of debridement therapy should be made on an individual patient basis. It will be influenced by the general condition of the patient, the environment in which the patient is being nursed, access to therapies and the nurse's knowledge and skill.

References

Bale, S. (1997) A guide to wound debridement. *Journal of Wound Care* **6**: 4, 179–182.

Bale, S., Jones, V. (1997) *Wound Care Nursing: A patient-centred approach*. London: Balliere Tindall.

Bergstrom, N., Bennett, M.A., Carlson, C.E. et al. (1994) *Treatment of Pressure Ulcers: Clinical practice guideline 15*. Public Health Service Agency for Health Care Policy and Research (Pub 95-0652). Rockeville NJ: Department of Health and Human Services.

Campbell, D., Hellgren, L., Karlstrom, B., Vincent, J. (1987) Debriding ability of multi-enzyme preparation isolated from Antarctic krill (Euphausia Superba). *Experienca* **43**: 578–579.

Church, J. (1996) Biosurgery in wound healing. *Journal of Wound Care* **5**: 2, 51.

Cutting, K., Harding, K.G. (1994) Criteria for identifying wound infection. *Journal of Wound Care* **3**: 4, 198–201.

Dealey, C. (1994) *The Care of Wounds*. Oxford: Blackwell Scientific Publications.

Glyantsev, S.P., Adamyan, A.A., Sakaharov, I.Y. (1997) Crab collagenase in wound debridement. *Journal of Wound Care* **6**: 1, 13–16.

Goode, P.S. (1995) Consensus on wound debridement: A US perspective. *European Tissue Repair Society* **2**: 4, 104.

Heggers, J.P. (1998) Defining infection in chronic wounds: Methodology. *Journal of Wound Care* **7**: 9, 452–456.

Hess, C.T. (1995) *Nurses' Clinical Guide to Wound Care*. Springhouse NJ: Springhouse.

Jing, W. (1995) The action of collagenase. *European Tissue Repair Society* **2**: 4, 106.

Majeske, C. (1992) Reliability of wound surface area measurements. *Physical Therapist* **72**: 2, 138–141.

Marks, J., Hughes, L.E., Harding, K.G. et al. (1983) Prediction of healing time as an aid to the management of open granulating wounds. *World Journal of Surgery* **7**: 41–45.

Margolis, D.J., Berlin, J.A., Strom, B.L. (1999) Risk factors associated with the failure of a venous leg ulcer to heal. *Arch Dermatol* **135**, 920–926.

Martin, S.J., Corrado, O.J., Kaye, E.A. (1996) Enzymatic debridement for necrotic wounds. *Journal of Wound Care* **5**: 7, 310–311.

Melhuish, J.M., Plassmann, P., Harding, K.G. (1994) Circumference, area and volume of the healing wound. *Journal of Wound Care* **3**: 8, 380–384.

Miller, M., Dyson, M. (1996) *Principles of Wound Care.* London: Macmillan.

Morison, M., Moffatt, C.J., Bridel-Nixon, J., Bale, S. (1997) *A Colour Guide to the Nursing Management of Chronic Wounds.* London: Mosby.

Morison, M. (1992) *A Colour Guide to the Nursing Management of Wounds.* London: Wolfe.

Mulder, G.D. (1995) Cost-effective managed care: Gel versus wet-to-dry for debridement. *Ostomy Wound Management* **41**: 2, 68–74.

Plassmann, P., Melhuish, J.M., Harding, K.G. (1994a) Problems of assessing wound size. *Wound Repair and Regeneration* **2**: 1, 68.

Plassmann, P., Melhuish, J.M., Harding, K.G. (1994b) Methods of measuring wound size: A comparative study. *Wounds* **6**: 2, 54–61.

Resch, C.S., Kerner, M.C., Heggers, J.P. et al. (1988) Pressure sore volume measurement: A technique to document and record wound healing. *Journal of the American Geriatric Society* **36**: 5, 444–446.

Stotts, N. (1995) Determination of bacterial burden in wounds. *Advances in Wound Care* **8**: 8, 46–52.

Thomas, S., Fear, M., Humphreys, J. (1994) Assessment of patients with chronic wounds. *Journal of Wound Care* **3**: 3, 151–154.

Thomas, S., Jones, M., Shutler, S., Jones, S. (1996) Using larvae in modern wound management. *Journal of Wound Care* **5**: 2, 60–69.

Thomas, S. (1990) *Wound Management and Dressing.* London: The Pharmaceutical Press.

5. Dressings and antiseptics

Sue Bale and David Leaper

Nurses are faced with an ever-expanding range of treatment modalities, and must choose the most appropriate treatment for the individual patient. Ritualistic practice, with no firm research basis, is no longer acceptable in nursing; increasingly, in all aspects of practice, evidence of the efficacy of therapies is being sought. It is however, difficult to generate research evidence on dressings and some other related wound treatments, due to the complexity of the disease processes found in patients with chronic wounds, and the large sample size required to adequately demonstrate statistically significant differences between treatments.

Dressing characteristics

The development of modern dressing technology is based on the principle of providing a moist wound/dressing interface. The theory of moist wound healing was first described by Winter (1962), who reported the results of a study to determine the rate of re-epithelialisation in pigs under dry and moist conditions. Winter observed that wounds treated with an occlusive dressing bathed the wound surface with exudate and healed faster than those left dry to form a scab.

A number of other functions have since been recommended as the characteristics that a good wound dressing should provide. The earliest of these by Turner (1982), and a more recent example by Bale and Morison (1997) are listed in Boxes 5.1 and 5.2.

In order to select the most appropriate material, nurses need to know and understand the physical properties and functions of each one. In conjunction with a thorough assessment of the patient, the wound and the environment (Bale and Jones, 1997), this knowledge will enable them to identify the best available treatment for that patient. In order to

---

Box 5.1 Characteristics of the ideal wound dressing (Turner, 1982)

- To maintain high humidity at the wound/dressing interface
- To remove excess exudate
- To allow gaseous exchange
- To provide thermal insulation
- To be impermeable to bacteria
- To be free of particles and toxic wound contaminants
- To allow removal without causing trauma to the wound

Box 5.2 Characteristics of the ideal wound dressing: a synthesis (Bale and Morrison, 1997)

- Non-adherent
- Impermeable to bacteria
- Capable of maintaining a high humidity at the wound site while removing excess exudate
- Thermally insulating
- Non-toxic and non-allergenic
- Comfortable and conformable
- Capable of protecting the wound from further trauma
- Requires infrequent dressing changes
- Cost-effective
- Long shelf life
- Available both in hospital and in the community

improve care and promote rational choices, many health trusts have developed policies to help nurses select dressings and other wound treatments, together with guidelines on their application and use.

The Drug Tariff (UK)

Not all dressings and devices available in hospital are available in the community and *vice versa*. The Drug Tariff is a list of all drugs, dressings, bandages, devices and equipment that can be prescribed by a GP and dispensed by a community pharmacist and reimbursed by the government. Updated regularly, the tariff states the prices reimbursed to community pharmacists, and is the method by which the NHS controls spending in the community. A wide range of dressings and bandages is now available on prescription from the GP for the management of a variety of wound aetiologies. However, it has been described as subjecting community practitioners to 'outdated rules and prejudices' (Heenan, 1999).

The types of dressing materials currently available across all settings are outlined below, together with recommendations for use. This is by no means a comprehensive list, but addresses the groups generically, with some examples for clarification.

Dressing types

Low-adherent wound contact dressings

These are relatively cheap and widely available (Box 5.3; Figure 5.1). Their function is to allow transmission of exudate through to secondary dressings whilst keeping the wound bed moist.

- **Multilayer/perforated plastic film (e.g. Melolin®, Telfa®)**
  These were the first absorbent dressings designed to reduce adherence to the wound bed.
- **Textile dressings (e.g. NA Ultra®, Tegapore®, Tricotex®)**
  These are suitable for a wide range of lightly- to heavily-exuding wounds. They are particularly useful for patients with sensitive or fragile skin.
- **Silicone (e.g. Mepital®)**
  This is suitable for patients with a wide range of lightly to heavily exuding wounds. Again, they are useful for patients with sensitive or fragile skin.

Film dressings

One of the earliest of the modern dressings to be developed, films provide a transparent primary wound cover with a range of fluid-handling capacities, depending on the brand (Figure 5.2). Examples of film dressings include OpSite® and Tegaderm®. They are extremely versatile and can be used both as primary and secondary dressings. When used as secondary dressings, films hold primary dressings in place and maintain a semi-occlusive environment. Their flexibility makes them ideal for application over joints and other body areas where conformability presents a problem.

Medicated materials

Dressings containing antiseptics and other antimicrobial agents are useful for patients with heavily colonised wounds or in situations where an aim of treatment is to reduce a

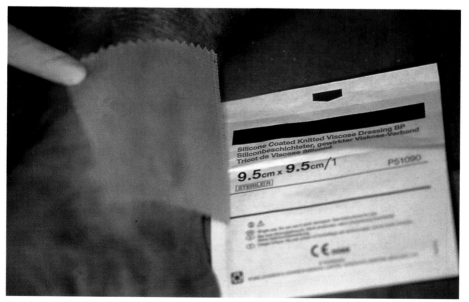

Figure 5.1 Low-adherent wound contact dressings allow transmission of exudate while keeping the wound bed moist

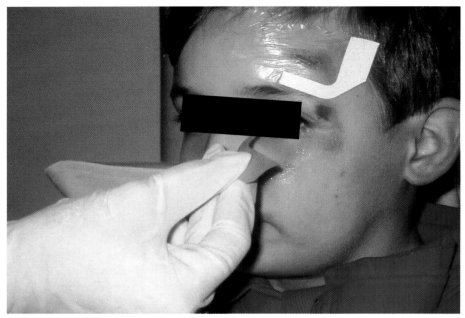

Figure 5.2 A film dressing used as a primary dressing

wound's bacterial load. The types of carriers used includes textiles, gels, creams, alginates and films to deliver:

- Silver-containing substances
- Iodine preparations
- Metronidazole.

Actisorb Plus®, Arglaes Alginate®, Arglaes Film®, Flamazine®, Inadine®, Iodosorb® and Metrotop Gel® are all examples of this diverse group.

Hydrogels

Hydrogels are composed of insoluble polymers which interact with aqueous solutions, so absorbing and retaining water. Amorphous hydrogels are the most commonly used gels and are presented as a viscous gel. These are applied directly to the wound bed and held in place by an occlusive or semi-occlusive dressing to maintain a moist environment at the wound surface. The levels of water donation and fluid absorption vary between brands. Hydrogels are used to maintain a moist environment to facilitate wound debridement through autolysis (Thomas and Leigh, 1998). It is suggested that by rehydrating devitalised tissue, phagocytic and enzymatic action is encouraged by autolytic debridement, so separating non-viable from healthy tissue.

Hydrogels are versatile dressings and can be used for a wide range of aetiologies, wound shapes and wound beds. Examples of hydrogels include Aquaform®, IntraSite Gel®, Nu-gel®, Purilon® and Sterigel®.

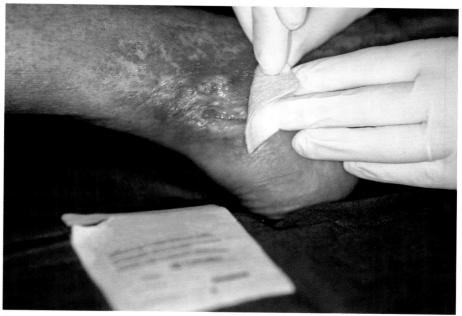

Figure 5.3 An alginate dressing being applied to a leg ulcer

Alginates

Derived from seaweed, alginate dressings are a combination of mannuronic acid and guluronic acid which form a polysaccharide material (Thomas and Leigh, 1998). They are available in a range of sheets and packing ropes for use on exuding wounds (Figure 5.3). On contact with exudate alginates gel at the wound/dressing interface. The haemostatic action of some alginates probably results from an exchange of calcium ions with sodium in the blood, leading to coagulation.

Alginate ropes and packing can be used to pack cavities, undermining, sinuses and tracts, while the sheets are used for flat wounds. Some manufacturers have bonded an absorbent pad for increased absorbency. Examples of alginates include Algisite M®, Algosteril®, Comfeel Seasorb®, Kaltogel®, Kaltostat®, Melgisorb®, Sorbsan® and Tegagen®.

Hydrocolloids

For the most part, hydrocolloid dressings consist of a thin sheet of foam or film with a sodium carboxymethylcellulose material bonded onto it (Figure 5.4). Gelatin, pectin, elastomers and adhesives are also used to give a flat, occlusive, adhesive dressing. Being mainly occlusive, hydrocolloids form a barrier to both liquids and bacteria, making them extremely useful for patients who wish to carry out normal daily activities without disturbing the wound bed or risking contamination of the wound. Used to treat a wide variety of wound types, hydrocolloids can remain *in situ* for several days without the

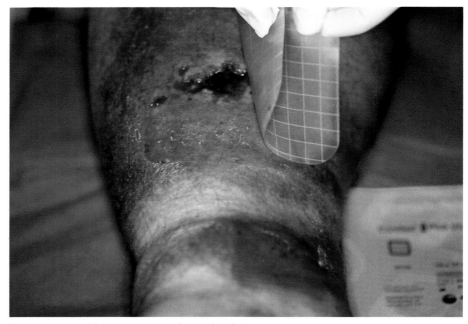

Fig 5.4 A hydrocolloid dressing being applied to a leg ulcer

need for absorbent secondary padding. Hydrocolloid gels and fibres are also available to treat more heavily exuding wounds, cavities, undermining, sinuses and tracts. These can then be covered with a hydrocolloid sheet to provide a convenient occlusive dressing. Comfeel Plus®, Granuflex® and Tegasorb® are examples of hydrocolloid sheets. Granugel® is a hydrocolloid gel and Aquacel® a hydrocolloid-based fibre, recently described as a hydrofibre.

Foams

Modern foam materials are absorbent, the level of absorbency depending on the type of dressing. Foams are a diverse group of dressings, both in terms of indication and presentation; they have been described as:
- Providing thermal insulation
- Not shedding particles
- Being easily cut or shaped
- Maintaining a moist environment
- Gas-permeable
- Non-adherent
- Light and comfortable to wear
- Absorbent (Thomas and Leigh (1998).

Adhesive, highly absorbent sheet foam dressings can be occlusive and can remain *in situ* for around four days. These products are useful for areas where dressing retention is

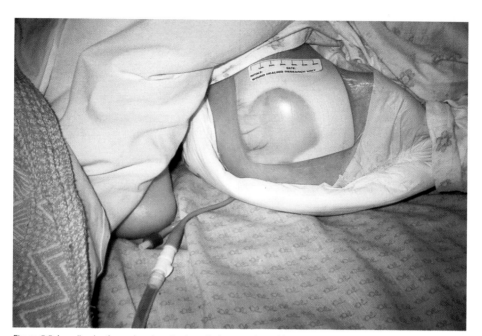

Figure 5.5 An adhesive foam dressing sheet applied to a patient with a heavily exuding pressure ulcer

difficult, as they require no additional adhesives or padding (Figure 5.5). Foams are available in shapes to cover the sacrum and heel, and where incontinence is present, they can protect the wound from contamination and so reduce the risk of infection. Examples of this group include Allevyn Adhesive®, Biatain®, Lyofoam Extra Adhesive® and Tielle Plus®.

Non-adhesive versions of some foams are also available, and are mainly used for patients with fragile or sensitive skin, commonly encountered with leg ulceration. Cotton retention bandages and compression bandages are used to secure dressings. Examples include Allevyn® and Lyofoam Extra®.

For cavity wounds, two types of foam are available. Allevyn Cavity Wound Dressing consists of small chips of hydrophilic polyurethane foam enclosed in a membrane of perforated polymeric film, forming a loosely-filled bag. In order to help meet individual patients' needs, a range of sizes and shapes are manufactured. Several dressings can be used together, in a combination of sizes and shapes. They can be inserted into, folded, applied in any orientation or inserted under skin undermining (Figure 5.6). They are is easily applied and have the added benefit of being disposable.

Cavi-Care® was invented in the early 1970s and first described for use on pilonidal sinus excision (Woods and Hughes, 1975). The product has since been redesigned and reformulated. A base and catalyst are mixed together in equal proportions to form a liquid which is poured into a cavity wound. After around two minutes the foam mixture

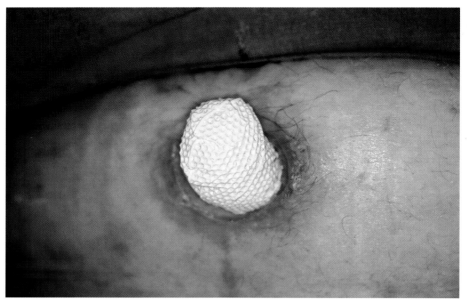

Figure 5.6 Allevyn Cavity Wound Dressing used to fill a deep pressure ulcer

expands and sets to form a soft, spongy cast (stent) of the wound; this exactly matches the shape and contours of the cavity, is non-adherent and absorbent. A reusable product, Cavi-Care® requires careful disinfection twice daily to ensure that bacterial counts remain low. At approximately weekly intervals (as the wound progresses towards healing and so changes shape) a new stent is poured. Research suggests that Cavi-Care® is easily managed by patients, relatives and carers, so reducing the need for nursing input at dressing changes (Bale et al., 1986). Where weekly wound assessment is appropriate and patients are willing and able to undertake routine wound and dressing cleansing, Cavi-Care can be extremely useful. It is contraindicated for wounds of poor shape including:

- those with narrow opening
- sinuses
- tracts
- extensive undermining
- very heavily exuding wounds.

When used in such situations there is a risk that the expanded foam could become retained in the wound.

Whatever dressing material is chosen, nurses transferring patients between settings should, as a matter of course, inform their colleagues of the current treatments being used. They should also attempt to ensure that there is no unnecessary disruption to a wound treatment programme, particularly when selecting dressings for hospital patients likely to need continuing treatment after discharge.

Antiseptic use in open wound management

The first antiseptic used in modern surgical practice was phenol. Lister, who introduced it in the 19th century, showed convincingly that compound fractures need not become infected and that amputation could be avoided. Antiseptic surgery was soon replaced by aseptic surgical techniques, but antiseptics have remained important parts of the surgical handwashing/skin preparation routine (see Chapter 7).

Various types of antibiotics have been used since ancient times to 'aid' healing by secondary intention. The Egyptians and ancient Greeks left many ideas for wound cleansing, which included natural substances of plant (sugar, wine, saps and resins), animal (honey, milk, urine and dung) and mineral (metal pigments) origin. Since Lister's time many less noxious antiseptics have been introduced, but all still tend to have toxic effects on living cells.

The use of antiseptics in the case of wounds healing by secondary intention has been the subject of recent reviews; debate and controversy have centred on the use of the disinfectant hypochlorite solutions. The subject has caused heated confrontations between healthcare professionals, and thanks to the campaigning of nurse practitioners hypochlorites have been virtually banned in many hospitals. While there is no doubt that hypochlorites are excellent disinfectants for use on working surfaces, lavatories and sluices, and to sterilise baby feeding bottles, experimental evidence suggests they should be used with caution on open wounds (Rodeheaver, 1997). Their efficacy when used as debriding agents cannot be denied; however, they are clearly toxic to healing tissues. As Flemming (1919) stated: 'It is necessary in the estimation of the value of an antiseptic to study its effect on the tissues more than its effect on the bacteria'.

Hypochlorites

A number of hypochlorites is available. Edinburgh University Solution of Lime (EUSOL) (chlorinated lime and boric acid solution), is a solution of chlorinated lime and boric acid with a pH of 7.5–8.5. The medical military need for a strong antiseptic to combat infection in the battlefield led to the development of Dakin's solution (surgical chlorinated soda solution) which was reported to have a dramatic effect in reducing wound sepsis (Dakin, 1915). Although clinical evidence of the efficacy of hypochlorite solutions remains anecdotal, they did become an established part of wound care; it would be interesting to see whether they would pass the strict regulations governing clinical trials if they were introduced today. When these antiseptics were introduced there was clearly a need for a cheap, effective topical antimicrobial and debriding agent, although it is interesting to note that Trueta (1939) managed compound fractures and open wounds very effectively using a closed method, without any antimicrobals at all.

The hypochlorites are unstable solutions which are easily inactivated by contact with organic substances. They are effective debriding agents, although their action is probably through damage to surface layers of living tissue, and are widely used prior to skin grafting. There are, however, equally effective alternative methods of cleaning necrotic wounds. Other antiseptics which do not damage living tissue, such as iodines, are effective with a wide spectrum of organisms. While the clinical use of hypochlorites has been well reviewed and argued, it still awaits proper clinical trials.

The experimental evidence against hypochlorites is based on their cytotoxicity on fibroblasts, white blood cells and endothelial cells in culture; the delay caused in healing of open wounds healing by secondary intention (measured by levels of hydroxyproline or prolonged inflammation); and their effects in the rabbit ear chamber, where vasoconstriction, cessation of blood flow and tissue death can be observed (Brennan and Leaper, 1985).

Silver sulphadiazine

Silver sulphadiazine is available as a cream for topical application to wounds. It is effective against a broad range of organisms, especially *Pseudomonas aeruginosa* and *Staphylococcus aureus*. Used initially as a burns therapy with success, silver sulphadiazine cream is increasingly being used on contaminated and colonised wounds. Mertz et al. (1997) recommend silver sulphadiazine for the treatment of chronic wounds colonised with *Pseudomonas aeruginosa* to reduce bacterial levels and so the risk of deep-seated infection.

Povidone iodine

Aqueous-free iodine is corrosive and stains tissues. Povidone iodine is a polyvinylpyrrolidine iodophor, presented with a detergent as Betadine, in various concentrations. The 10% aqueous form is equivalent to 1% free iodine. Iodine can aggravate thyroid diseases (Hashimoto's thyroiditis, Grave's disease and non-toxic nodular goitre), and its use is contra-indicated in these patients. Dilute solutions are probably effective for use as topical antimicrobials but without the risk of tissue damage.

There is some evidence that povidone iodine reduces infection in lacerations and it is an effective skin preparation and hand-washing agent (Lilly et al., 1982). However, in open wounds it should be used with caution as it may actually increase infection and delay healing. In experimental studies povidone iodine has been shown to inhibit white blood cell and fibroblast growth in cell culture, and to reduce the acquisition of tensile strength in healing wounds (Deas et al., 1986).

Cadexomer iodine

Cadexomer iodine is a modified starch to which iodine is physically bound. The starch absorbs exudate and releases iodine into the wound. Cadexomer iodine has a broad spectrum of activity against Gram positive and negative bacteria, fungi and protozoa. As with other iodine preparations, caution must be taken with patients with thyroid disease.

A consensus meeting debated the use of iodine in wound care (Gilchrist, 1997) and concluded that many concerns about its toxicity was related to old formulations. Newer preparations are reported to be safe and have useful antimicrobial properties, and are thought to be effective in debridement.

Chlorhexidine

Chlorhexidine is effective as a hand-washing agent and for skin preparation. It is widely used for pre-operative bathing or showering, although there is no proven clinical benefit to this. Chlorhexidine does, however, have a prolonged broad spectrum of activity against Gram positive and negative organisms. It is a useful alternative to povidone iodine in cases of hypersensitivity, and cannot be absorbed through intact skin. Chlorhexidine is less affected by body fluids, and has been shown to be superior to other antiseptics in terms of its microbial action (Brennan and Leaper, 1985). It is not exempt from toxic effects in tissues but has not been assessed as fully as other antiseptics.

Hydrogen peroxide

Hydrogen peroxide is widely used as a wound irrigant. However, oxygen bubbles are released when it comes in contact with non-epithelialised tissue; these may damage tissue, and there is a risk of bubble embolus. There is no evidence of antimicrobial activity, nor is hydrogen peroxide toxic in rabbit ear chamber evaluation (Brennan and Leaper, 1985). Although hydrogen peroxide does not appear to interfere with healing, it is toxic to fibroblasts.

References

Bale, S., Creese, A., Harding, K.G., Hughes, L.E. (1986) *The Practitioner* **5**: 2, 632–639.

Bale, S., Jones, V. (1997) *Wound Care Nursing: A patient-centred approach.* London: Balliere Tindall.

Bale, S., Morison, M. (1997) Wound dressings. In: Morison, M., Moffat, C., Bridel-Nixon, J. et al. *A Colour Guide to the Nursing Management of Chronic Wounds.* London: Mosby.

Brennan, S.S., Leaper, D.J. (1985) The effect of antiseptics on the healing wound: A study using the rabbit ear chamber. *British Journal of Surgery* **72**: 780–782.

Dakin, H.D. (1915) On the use of certain antiseptic substances in the treatment of infected wounds. *British Medical Journal* **2**: 318–320.

Deas, J., Billings, P., Brennan, S.S. et al. (1986) The toxicity of commonly used antiseptics on fibroblasts in tissue culture. *Phlebology*; **1**: 205–209.

Gilchrist, B. (1997) Should iodine be considered in wound management? *Journal of Wound Care* **6**: 3, 148–151.

Heenan, A. (1999) Wound dressings and the Drug Tariff. *Journal of Wound Care* **8**: 2, 69–72.

Flemming, A. (1919) The action of chemical and physiological antiseptics in a septic wound. *British Journal of Surgery* 1919; **7**: 99–129.

Lilly, H.A., Lombury, E.J.L., White, W. et al. (1982) The effect of ultra clean air in operative wounds on deep sepsis in the joint after total hip or knee replacement: a randomised study. *British Medical Journal* **285**: 10–14.

Mertz, P.M., Davis, S.C., Olivier-Gandi, G.M., Eaglestein, W.H. (1997) The wound environment: Implications from research studies for healing and infection. In: Krasner, D., Kane, D. (eds) *Chronic Wound Care* (2nd edn). Wayne Pa: health Management Publications.

Morison, M., Moffatt, C. (1997) Leg ulcers. In: Morison, M., Moffatt, C., Bridel-Nixon, J., Bale, S. (eds). *A Colour Guide to the Nursing Management of Chronic Wounds.* London: Mosby.

Rodeheaver, G.T. 1997. Wound cleansing, wound irrigation, wound disinfection. In: Krasner, D., Kane, D. *Chronic Wound Care* (2nd edn). Wayne, PA, Health Management Publications Inc.

Thomas, S., Leigh, I. (1998) Wound dressings. In: Leaper, D.J., Harding, K.G. (eds). *Wounds: Biology and management.* Oxford: Oxford University Press.

Trueta, J. (1939) Closed treatment of war fractures. *Lancet* i: 1452–1455.

Turner, T.D. (1982) Which dressing and why? *Nursing Times* **78**: 29 (suppl.), 1–3.

Winter, G.D. (1962) Formation of scab and the rate of epithelialisation of superficial wounds in the skin of the domestic pig. *Nature* **193**: 293–294.

Woods, R.A.B., Hughes, L.E. (1975) Silicone foam sponge for pilonidal sinus: a new technique for dressing open granulating wounds. *British Medical Journal* **3**, 131–133.

6. Bandages and other therapies

Sue Bale and David Leaper

Bandages are defined by their performance characteristics and are thus classified into three groups (Thomas and Nelson, 1998). In clinical practice also bandages have several uses based on their performance in terms of providing support and compression:

Type 1: conformable, light bandages used as a means of retaining primary dressings; examples include Easifix, K-Band and Slinky (Figure 6.1)

Type 2: light support or short-stretch inelastic bandages

Type 3: elastic compression bandages, which provide a range of strengths of pressure.

The theory of and indications for use of compression bandages are described in Chapter 8. For the management of patients with venous ulceration two main types of bandage are available, elastic and non-elastic.

Elastic bandages

Elastic compression bandages exert sustained pressure on the leg, helping to support a defective venous system and reduce oedema. Four sub-classes of Type 3 elastic compression bandage are available

Class 3a: low levels of pressure, up to 17mmHg at the ankle

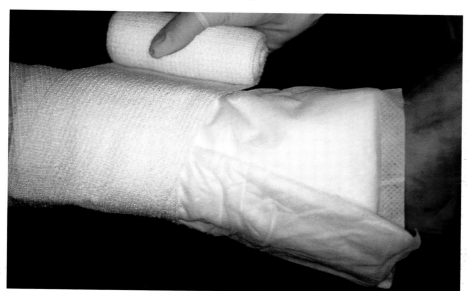

Figure 6.1 Type 1 bandages can be used to retain primary dressings

Class 3b: moderate to high levels of pressure, up to 24mmHg at the ankle

Class 3c: high levels of pressure, 35mmHg at the ankle

Class 3d: very high levels of pressure, 50mmHg at the ankle.

In the UK, for most patients with venous leg ulceration, oedema reduction is achieved with a Class 3c bandage.

Most 10cm wide compression bandages are applied with a 50% overlap and at 50% extension. It can take time to develop the skills required to achieve the correct extension, but some manufacturers provide a visual aid to help the user, such as a printed rectangle or oval throughout the bandage (which when stretched by 50% becomes a square or a circle respectively). Manufacturers' recommendations come with each individual bandage and provide information on limb size, application and use of visual aids as well as washing instructions and life expectancy of the bandage. In general, bandages should be hand-washed in pure soap (e.g. Lux or Fairy), dried away from direct heat and light and used for around 20 washes, depending on the brand. The performance of a bandage depends not only on it being applied correctly but also on washing, drying and anticipated life expectancy.

Multi-layer systems

The Charing Cross four-layer bandage system, and variations on it (Profore, K-Four), are popular methods of applying sustained compression for periods of up to a week (Figure 6.2). This system comprises of:
- Orthopaedic wool to pad bony prominences
- Crêpe to form a smooth base
- A lightweight elastomeric bandage to provide light compression
- A cohesive bandage to provide additional compression.

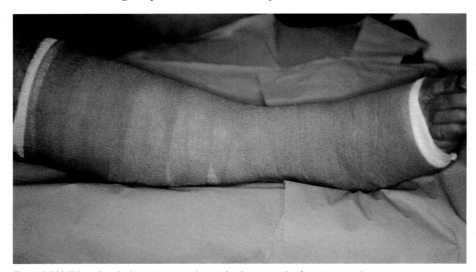

Figure 6.2 Multi-layer bandaging systems apply sustained compression for up to a week

Pressures of 42mmHg at the ankle have been reported with the four-layer system (Moffatt and Dickson, 1993). The original Charing Cross work formed the foundation for community leg ulcer clinics (Moffatt et al., 1992), defining a standard for healing as normally 70% at 12 weeks in this setting (Blair et al., 1988). This seminal work also led to the development of formal training in lower-limb assessment for community nurses. Moffatt's work in particular has resulted in significant change in the care received by patients with leg ulceration, which has led to improved ulcer healing rates (Moffatt et al., 1992). Moffatt also achieved improvements in patients' quality of life and a reduction in the cost of ulcer management within her health authority (Moffatt and Dickson, 1993).

High compression may not be suitable for all patients with venous leg ulceration, for a number of reasons:

- Some find it difficult to tolerate the compression, and this results in poor compliance; these patients are then often treated with a bandage system that produces lower pressure than the ideal
- Those with new ulceration must await the results of investigations to confirm venous disease
- Some newly ulcerated patients are nervous of being treated with high compression
- In patients with a wound infection producing pain, reduced compression may be indicated for a short time, whilst the infection is treated.

These patients present a difficult clinical problem. Where high compression is not an option the patient may be introduced gradually to compression therapy in several ways:

- The use of paste bandage with light compression
- Single-layer tubular bandages
- Three layers of differing length tubular bandages
- Class 3c bandages applied at less than 50% extension.

Once a patient is comfortable and confident wearing support or light compression, a higher level of compression might be considered. As the pain of oedema reduces with compression therapy, patients may be happy to proceed to higher levels of compression.

Inelastic bandages

Short-stretch or inelastic bandages provide minimal stretch and, once applied, form a semi-rigid cylinder of bandage (Figure 6.3). In the active, ambulant patient, the calf muscle pushes against the bandages,

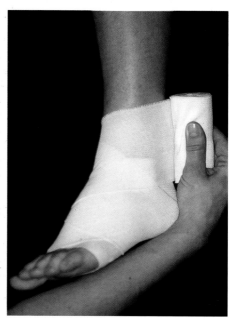

Figure 6.3 Inelastic bandages form a semi-rigid column

65

Box 6.1 Effective bandaging regimens
(Thomas and Nelson, 1988)

Non-elastomeric regimens	**Healing rates**
Two-layer compression Paste bandage and Coban® (Unna's boot)	64% in 15 weeks
Padding and 'short-stretch', for example, Rosidal K®	71% in three months
Three-layer compression Paste (woven cotton bandage), Elastocrêpe® and shaped tubular bandage	66% in three months
Padding, short-stretch and Coban®	60% in one year
Elastomeric regimens	
Two-layer compression Lining sock and compression sock	84% in three months
Three-layer compression Wool, Tensopress® and shaped tubular bandage	54% in three months
Paste, Tensopress® and shaped tubular bandage	64% in three months
Four-layer compression Wool, crêpe, Elset® (or equivalent) and Coban® (or equivalent)	From 22–74% in three months to 60% in one year
Tubifast®, lint and Setopress®	44% in three months
Paste, Elastocrêpe®, Elastoplast® and Class 2 stocking	60% in three months

achieving very high pressures which quickly reduce oedema. During the first few days of wearing these bandages often need frequent reapplication as oedema is rapidly reduced. Although widely used throughout Europe as a first-line treatment for oedema, in the UK elastic compression tends to be the treatment of choice. The effectiveness of bandaging regimens has been reviewed (Thomas and Nelson, 1998) and is summarised in Box 6.1.

Compression hosiery

Although full-leg compression stockings are available, for ease of use, patients generally prefer below-knee hosiery, which are just as effective for most patients (Morison and Moffatt, 1997). As with bandages, different levels of compression are available:

Level 1: low levels of pressure, 14–17mmHg at the ankle

Level 2: medium levels of pressure, 18–24mmHg at the ankle

Level 3: high levels of pressure, 25–35mmHg at the ankle.

For patients whose ulcers are small and lightly exuding and who do not require secondary dressings and absorbent padding, hosiery may be a preferred form of compression (Figure 6.4).

In the UK compression hosiery is mainly used as preventative therapy following healing of venous ulcers. Although the evidence to support the use of compression hosiery is weak there has been some documentation of the recurrence rates of ulceration, which are reported to be 16–30% (Keachie, 1995).

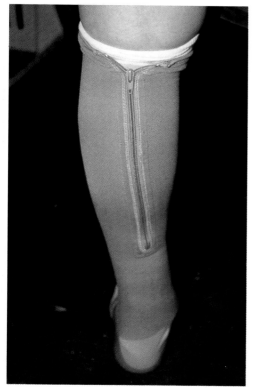

Fig 6.4 Compression hosiery is suitable where secondary dressings and absorbent padding are not required

The lifespan of hosiery, as with bandages, is limited, and again, hand-washing in pure soap and drying away from direct heat is required. Depending on the brand and the manufacturer's instructions hosiery should be effective for 3–6 months.

Patient compliance is the main problem related to the use or otherwise of compression hosiery (Keachie, 1995); poor compliance is caused by a number of problems:

- inability to get them on and off, due to arthritic hands, poor eyesight, ill-fitting design or poor dexterity
- lack of professional input to educate, support, and help to apply and change hosiery
- forgetfulness — once their ulcer has healed, few patients receive professional support to reinforce the need for continuing compression
- the hosiery feels too warm, too tight or uncomfortable.

Intermittent compression devices

Intermittent compression is used to treat lymphoedema but can also be used for patients with venous disease. A pneumatic boot is applied to the leg and zipped in place, and the device gently massages fluid through the lymphatic system. This system is recommended as an adjunctive therapy to compression bandaging (Coleridge-Smith et al., 1990).

The intermittent compression device can be used at home and is usually applied twice daily for at least one hour, in the morning and evening. The device can be set for a range of cycle times and pressures.

Vacuum-assisted closure®

Vacuum-assisted closure therapy® (KCI International) is based on the principle of applying negative pressure to the wound bed. It is thought that this stimulates blood flow to the wound bed so encouraging angiogenesis and healing. The device consists of a polyurethane foam pack that is inserted into the wound and covered with a film (to provide an air-tight seal). Suction at a level of 125mmHg is applied via tubing into the foam dressing; exudate drained from the wound bed is collected in a container. Suction can be applied either continuously or intermittently. The intermittent regimen has been described by Deva et al. (1997); 125mmHg suction was applied in cycles of five minutes of suction and two minutes rest. It has been used on a range of chronic and acute wound aetiologies (Argenta and Morykwas, 1997) and as a preparation for plastic surgery (Blackburn et al., 1998).

Warm-Up®

Wound temperature is thought to directly influence tissue oxygenation, which is associated with resistance to infection and healing (Hopf, 2000) and the rate of cell division. Normal human tissues have been described by Ryan (2000) as having a metabolism finely adapted to 37°C. Warm-Up® (Augustine Medical) aims to maintain the wound and peri-wound skin as near to 37°C as possible. It delivers radiant heat to the wound bed and maintains that warmth, together with humidity, using a non-contact dressing applied over the wound. Warm-Up® has been used on patients with a variety of chronic wounds including leg ulcers, pressure ulcers and diabetic foot ulcers (Phillips and Park, 1998; Berman and Dumit-Minkel, 1998).

Other therapies

In other countries, especially the USA, physiotherapists have a well-established role in wound care. They offer a range of therapies including electric stimulation, hydrotherapy, low-intensity laser, ultrasound and ultraviolet light (McCulloch, 1998). Evidence of clinical efficacy for the most part is weak, and randomised controlled studies are required (Gogia, 1997).

Recent developments in wound treatment

A fuller understanding of the mechanisms of human wound healing is leading to the development of a whole host of new treatments, including:
- Growth factors
- Living skin equivalents

Growth factors

Growth factors or cytokines are polypeptide proteins which occur naturally in the body. Wound healing growth factors are produced by many cells including platelets and macrophages, and act as chemical messengers throughout the healing process. Although many have been discovered, as scientific research progresses, it is likely that others will follow. Different scientific disciplines (immunology, haematology and biochemistry) have been independently researching in this field, and this may be the reason for the confusing array of names for cytokines (Garrett and Garrett, 1997).

Growth factors are naturally produced in small amounts by humans, so topical application to wounds is normally only possible by using genetic engineering (Garrett and Garrett, 1997). The topical treatment of wounds with growth factors aims to correct or compensate for delayed healing in difficult or chronic wounds when healing is not progressing. Hart (1999) describes the actions of a range of growth factors that have been subjected to clinical evaluation. These include basic fibroblast growth factor (bFGF), transforming growth factor-ß2 (TGF-ß2), platelet-derived growth factor-BB (PDGF-BB), epidermal growth factor (EGF), and interleukin-1ß (IL-1ß). Box 6.2 shows the actions of various growth factors in wound healing (Arnold et al., 1995).

The wound healing process is extremely complex, and a wide range of growth factors are beneficial; however, the choice of which to use on which aetiology and at what stage of healing has yet to be defined. The results of clinical research in patients with chronic wounds has been disappointing to date (Garrett and Garrett, 1997), though as the knowledge base is extended there is potential for the use of growth factors in clinical practice. The use of combinations of growth factors (which more closely mimic normal human wound healing) has been cited as the next step in their use (Fylling, 1997). As research proceeds, it is likely that the role and value of growth factors in the management of wounds will be clarified.

Tissue engineering

In the past, split thickness and full thickness skin grafts and sheets of keratinocytes (grown from a section of the patient's own skin) have been used to treat deep and extensive burns. Developments in this field have resulted in more sophisticated and readily available skin replacements that have been manufactured or engineered. Although not recommended for routine clinical use, these technologies offer a treatment for patients with difficult wounds which are resistant to conventional dressing treatment. These wounds include chronic leg, diabetic and pressure ulcers, and other recalcitrant

---

Box 6.2 Growth factors in wound healing (Arnold et al., 1995)

Cytokine	Abbreviation	Producer cells	Primary actions
Platelet-derived growth factor	PDGF	Platelets, macrophages	Angiogenesis, fibroplasia
Transforming growth factor-β	TGF-β	Platelets, macrophages	Matrix synthesis
Fibroblast growth factor	FGF	Fibroblasts	Angiogenesis
Vasoactive endothelial growth factor	VEGF	Keratinocytes	Angiogenesis
Insulin-like growth factor-1	IGF-1	Fibroblasts, endothelium, macrophages	Fibroplasia
Epidermal growth factor	EGF	Keratinocytes	Epithelialisation
Transforming growth factor-α	TGF-α	Keratinocytes	Epithelialisation
Endothelin-1	En-1	Endothelium	Contraction
Interferon-γ	IFN-γ	Lymphocytes	Wound maturation
Interleukin-4	IL-4	Lymphocytes	Fibroplasia
Monocyte-colony stimulating factor	M-CSF	Macrophages, ?other	Monocytes migration and maturation
Granulocyte monocyte-colony stimulating factor	GM-CSF	Macrophages, ?other	Monocytes migration and maturation

wounds where other therapies have failed. There are two sources of skin replacement: autologous is from the patient's own skin, allogenic is from other humans.

Mulder (1999) reviewed the role of tissue engineering in skin care and identified four types of engineered skin:

1. Human allograft-derived product (Alloderm Processed Allograft Dermis, Life-Cell Corporation). This comes from cadaver skin and is obtained from skin banks. The skin is treated and processed to remove cells that would stimulate an immune response and so lead to rejection, and is then freeze-dried and stored ready for use. Mulder (1999) suggests that for burns and plastic surgery this type of product has been successful. However, it has yet to show benefits for patients with chronic ulceration.

2. Cultured human keratinocytes. Keratinocytes are cultured in the laboratory and grown on transport sheets. Being a single-cell product they are most useful in the treatment of burns and partial thickness wounds. Deeper, full thickness wounds have been difficult to treat with keratinocytes — Mulder suggests that this could be due to the lack of viable dermis onto which the keratinocytes can adhere.

3. **Human dermal replacement** (Dermagraft, Joint Venture – Advanced Tissue Sciences/ Smith & Nephew). This is derived from human neonatal foreskins, discarded after circumcision. It contains fibroblasts, living cells which are cultured on a bioabsorbable sheet. This product can be used to replace lost dermis and has been successfully used on patients with diabetic foot ulceration. On application the active fibroblasts deliver growth factors to the wound. Dermagraft is thought to stimulate healing by replacing the damaged tissue with a living healthy dermal tissue consisting of collagen, fibronectin, glycosaminoglycans and growth factors.

4. **Bilayered skin equivalent** (Apligraft, Organogenesis). This is a bio-engineered tissue consisting of a fully differentiated epidermis and a dermis. The epidermis is composed of cornified differentiated keratinocytes and a dermal matrix composed of a collagen lattice containing viable fibroblasts. It is similar in many ways to the patient's own skin, and is thought to stimulate healing by producing a range of growth factors.

Tissue engineered products are expensive. At present they are being evaluated and used in patients with difficult wounds that are resistant to healing, since managing these wounds is in itself expensive. Decisions on when and whether to use tissue engineered products are best made on an individual patient basis, balancing the long-term financial and personal costs of conventional treatment with the cost of tissue engineered treatment.

References

Argenta, L.C., Morykwas, M.J. (1997) Vacuum-assisted closure: A new method for wound control and treatment. *Annals of Plastic Surgery* **38**: 6, 563–576.

Arnold, F., O'Brien, J., Cherry, G. (1995) Granulocyte monocyte-colony stimulating factor as an agent for wound healing. *Journal of Wound Care* **4**: 9, 400–402.

Blair, S.D., Wright, D.D., Backhouse, C.M. et al. (1988) Sustained compression and healing of chronic ulcers. *British Medical Journal* **297**: 1159–1161.

Berman, J.E., Dumit-Minkel, P.T. (1998) *Effects of a Heated Dressing on Peri-wound Skin Temperature and Healing of Full-thickness Pressure Ulcers.* Second European Pressure Ulcer Advisory Panel Open Meeting, Oxford, England, September 1998.

Blackburn, J.H., Boemi, L., Hall, W.W. et al. (1998) Negative-pressure dressings as a bolster for skin grafts. *Annals of Plastic Surgery* **40**: 5, pp 453–457.

Coleridge-Smith, P., Sarin, S., Hasler, J. (1990) Sequential gradient pneumatic compression enhances venous leg ulcer healing: A randomised trial. *Surgery* **108**: 871–875.

Deva, A.K., Siu, C., Nettle, W.J.S. (1997) Vacuum-assisted closure of a sacral pressure sore. *Journal of Wound Care* **6**: 7, 311–312.

Fylling, C.P. (1997) Growth factors: a new era in wound healing. In: Krasner, D., Kane, D. (eds) *Chronic Wound Care* (2nd edn). Wayne Tx: Health Management Publications.

Garrett, B., Garrett, S.B. (1997) Cellular communication and the action of growth factors during wound healing. *Journal of Wound Care* **6**: 6, 277–280.

Gogia, P.P. (1997) Physical therapy in wound management. In: Krasner, D., Kane, D. (eds). *Chronic Wound Care* (2nd edn). Wayne Pa: Health Management Publications.

Hart, J. (1999) Growth factors. In: Miller, M., Glover, D. (eds) *Wound Management: Theory and practice*. London: Emap Healthcare Ltd.

Hopf, H. (2000) Role of warming and oxygen tension in wounds. In: Ryan, T.J., Cherry, G.W., Harding, K.G. (eds) *Warming and Wound Healing*. London: Royal Society of Medicine.

Keachie, J. (1995) Prevention of re-ulceration. In: Cullum, N., Roe. B. (eds) *Leg Ulcers: Nursing management*. Harrow: Scutari Press.

McCulloch, J., (1998) The role of physiotherapy in managing patients with acute wounds. *Journal of Wound Care* **7**: 5, 241–244.

Moffatt, C.J., Franks, P.J., Oldroyd, M. et al. (1992) Community clinics for leg ulcers and impact on healing. *British Medical Journal* **305**: 1389–1392.

Moffatt, C.J., Dickson, D. (1993) The Charing Cross high compression four-layer bandage system. *Journal of Wound Care* **2**: 2, 91–94.

Morison, M., Moffatt, C. (1997) Leg ulcers. In: Morison, M., Moffatt, C., Bridel-Nixon, J., Bale, S. (eds) *A Colour Guide to the Nursing Management of Chronic Wounds*. London: Mosby.

Mulder, G.T. (1999) The role of tissue engineering in wound care. *Journal of Wound Care* **8**:1, 21–24.

Phillips, T.J., Park, H.Y. (1998) *Heating Device Reduces the Growth Inhibitory Activity in Chronic Wound Fluid*. Symposium on Advanced Wound Care and Medical Research Forum on Wound Repair, Miami, Florida.

Ryan T.J. (2000) Warming the skin: A review. In: Ryan, T.J., Cherry, G.W., Harding, K.G. (eds) *Warming and Wound Healing*. London: Royal Society of Medicine.

Thomas, S., Nelson, E.A. (1998) Graduated external compression in the treatment of venous disease. In: Emap Healthcare. *The Science of Bandaging*. London: Emap Healthcare.

The Challenges of Specific Aetiologies

7. Acute wounds

Sue Bale and David Leaper

Traumatic wounds

Traumatic wounds cover a wide range of tissue injury, mostly accidental in origin, ranging from lacerations to burns and scalds. These aetiologies reflect those commonly presenting to accident and emergency (A&E) departments throughout the UK. The less common traumatic wounds, such as those resulting from battle injury, are not addressed here; information on their care and management can be found in specialised texts.

Most traumatic wounds result from accidents at work or home, less common are those related to road traffic accidents (RTAs), physical attack and animal bites. In 1989 about 317,000 people were injured in RTAs (CSO, 1990); although many such injuries are preventable, the wearing of crash helmets and use of seat belts has reduced their severity. Drinking and driving does, however, contribute to the incidence of head injury (Allen and Craig, 1994).

Patients presenting to A&E with traumatic wounds are from all age groups, and many are young and normally fit and healthy. In general a detailed history should be taken to assess how the injury happened, how dirty or contaminated the wound is, current medication and other underlying disease processes. The outcome of this history-taking will influence the way in which the wound is managed.

Traumatic lacerations

By the time a patient presents to A&E with a laceration, the wound is likely to be contaminated, so wound cleansing and/or debridement does not necessarily need to be undertaken using an aseptic technique. The main priorities in treating traumatic lacerations include wound cleansing, removal of all deeply embedded foreign bodies (using anaesthetics where appropriate), and assessment for damage to underlying nerves and tendons (Bale and Jones, 1997). Where extensive or deep injury is proven or suspected, further radiological investigations may be required. Other treatments that need to be considered include tetanus prophylaxis and antibiotic therapy.

Local wound care

Where the risk of infection is considered to be low and there is sufficient tissue, the wound edges may be sutured. The advantage of this technique is to restore physical and cosmetic function. However, if there is a possibility of gross contamination, or the wound edges cannot be brought together without causing tension in the tissues, it is advisable to leave the wound unsutured (Figure 7.1). For these wounds a range of dressings or modern materials can be used.

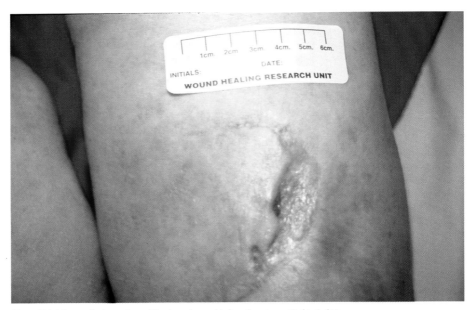

Figure 7.1 A traumatic laceration of the leg where skin loss has prevented suturing

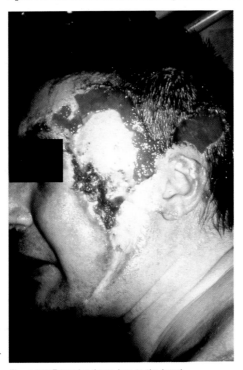

Figure 7.2 Extensive tissue loss to the head

Facial wounds

Due to their potential cosmetic impact facial wounds are covered here separately; plastic surgery is often indicated to produce the best cosmetic result possible. Lacerations are best sutured within eight hours of injury, although with thorough cleansing this can be extended to 48 hours without significantly increasing the risk of scarring and infection (Al-Khateeb et al., 1995). Special care should be taken to assess for damage to the facial nerve, as it is possible to repair damaged nerve ends within 72 hours of injury. This should be done using microsurgical techniques under magnification. Although some regeneration of nerves is possible, it is rare to effect a completely normal functioning of the damaged nerve (Al-Khateeb et al., 1995). Particular care should also be taken in repairing lacerations of the lip, the eyelid and orbital area.

In situations where tissue loss prevents primary closure, a range of plastic surgical techniques can be used to fill or cover such defects (Figure 7.2). These include free grafts, pedicle grafts or flaps, full and split thickness skin grafts.

Animal bites

These are the most common cause of facial injury, and in Western countries 90% are caused by dogs (Wishan and Huang, 1989). Children are the most commonly affected by dog bites, accounting for 50–75% of these injuries (Boenning et al., 1983) and the face is the most frequent site (80%) bitten (Lackmann et al., 1992). The risk of infection from a dog bite is extremely high; infective organisms include tetanus and rabies, though other pathogenic organisms are more commonly found in the dog's mouth. Plastic surgery is often required to repair facial injury, and sutures should be removed 4–5 days after surgery to prevent scarring from suture marks. Postoperatively, in the first three months of the healing phase, it is suggested these wounds need to avoid prolonged saturation with water and direct exposure to the sun (Holt, 1990).

Contusions and abrasions

These facial injuries are often associated with RTAs, and other more serious injury to the patient may be evident. Often gentle cleansing of the area and observations are all that is required. However, where grit and contaminants from the road surface are embedded in an abrasion, permanent scarring or 'tattooing' can occur. To prevent this, thorough cleansing by scrubbing the area is required to remove all the foreign bodies.

Sutured wounds

A number of factors related to clinical technique and environmental conditions can affect the success of surgery and the postoperative management of surgical wounds.

Antiseptics

The value of antiseptics is unquestioned for use in skin preparation: a single application of povidone iodine (Betadine®) or chlorhexidine reduces superficial skin flora by more than 95% (Lilly et al., 1982). For hand-washing on the wards, ordinary soap is sufficient for clean procedures, although aqueous antiseptic solutions can also be used; however, adequate drying of the skin with disposable towels is always important.

Prior to surgery and aseptic techniques, scrubbing of the fingernails only is required for the first procedure of the day, together with hand-washing to the elbows for five minutes. Subsequently hand-washing for two minutes is sufficient between operations, as excessive scrubbing or hand-washing can damage the skin and increase bacterial penetration; aqueous antiseptics such as povidone iodine, chlorhexidine, or triclosan are ideal for this purpose. Body washing with antiseptics prior to surgery is of questionable value.

The surgical environment

Theatre discipline is essential to minimise the incidence of infection. The use of modular theatres and exhaust operating suits for orthopaedic prosthetic surgery have been abandoned in favour of wound irrigation, ultraviolet light and prophylactic antibiotics, which are as effective in controlling infection. It is logical to ban patients and staff from the operating theatre if they have open infective skin lesions, while the flow of patients and instruments through a set plan (clean to dirty) is also logical: the patient moves from entrance corridor to anaesthetic room, operating theatre, to ward; instruments go from the central sterile supplies department to theatre, to sluice.

Protective clothing

There is no need for sticky pads to be placed on the floor at the theatre entrance, while the use of overshoes for staff bringing patients from the wards for surgery simply results in contaminated hands. Standard theatre gowns are made of light woven cotton or a similar synthetic material, but these do little to prevent transfer of marker organisms, such as the staphylococci. Disposable non-woven, non-weave, cellulose gowns are ideal when transfer of organisms is a risk (and for patients with a risk of hepatitis or HIV transfer); however, these are expensive and not as comfortable to wear. The use of gloves, masks and hair caps is also traditional but, together with incise drapes, wound guards, and drains, their value can be questioned.

Gloves are worn to protect the patient from any bacteria remaining on the hands of the operating team, although the risk is small and probably only significant in prosthetic surgery. Like gowns, however, gloves can also protect the operating team from viral infection which may be acquired from the patient.

Masks are necessary in prosthetic surgery, particularly in conjunction with hoods for those with long hair or a beard. There is little evidence that discarding the use of masks in non-prosthetic general surgery increases the risk of wound infection. Again, however, the mask can protect the operator from infected body fluids, particularly blood.

Incise drapes and wound guards

Adhesive polyurethane transparent films were introduced to secure operative drapes, avoid the use of towel clips and isolate stomas from a planned new wound. They are also widely used as wound dressings to cover sutured wounds, but there is little evidence that they reduce wound infections (Jackson et al., 1971). Incise drapes impregnated with antiseptics such as povidone iodine may lower the bacterial count at the skin surface but do not affect colonisation in the wound during an operation (Lewis et al., 1984). Wound guards, which are intended to protect the wound edges during an operative procedure, also seem to offer little protection against infection (Alexander Williams et al., 1972).

Sterile instruments

Most instruments can be resterilised by autoclaving after they have been cleaned and checked. This works through the penetrative action of steam under pressure. Delicate instruments, such as endoscopes, require sterilisation using an antiseptic such as glutaraldehyde; however, this is toxic, and safer alternatives are becoming available. Disposable materials, such as needles and sutures, can be mass sterilised in the manufacturer's plant using gamma-irradiation or ethylene oxide.

Appropriate suture materials and dressings

Suture materials are used to hold tissues together until healing is complete. By avoiding excessive trauma or use of diathermy, surgery should leave no dead tissue or foreign materials other than prosthetic implants and closure materials.

The use of suture material to hold tissues together until they are healed must be balanced with a number of factors. Too much effort to reduce the theoretical risk of dead space in the wound may increase tissue tension and still fail to prevent the collection of a haematoma or a later infection. Adequate perfusion of the wound, determined by local and systemic factors, is probably the best predictor of healing with reduction of infection. Sutures used for wound closure must be placed outside the biochemically active zone of the wound edge, or they will fail to hold the tissues together. This lytic zone is widened by infection but can be minimised by the use of the least reactive fine material (usually a synthetic, non-absorbable monofilament). No great strength is required in bowel anastomosis, which simply requires opposition, whereas great indefinite strength is required for vascular anastomosis. Appropriate sutures should be used for these tasks.

Drains

Drains are used to minimise dead space in the wound and to evacuate haematomas or body fluids, with the intention of reducing the risk of infection. There is no clear evidence of their effectiveness (Bartolo, 1985), but it is likely that they are used when there is a risk of wound breakdown or collection of fluid, more to appease a surgeon's conscience than anything else. Closed disposable suction drains are the most widely used (Harland and Gruing, 1988); their built-in valve prevents reflux of fluid and the inflow of external organisms which can occur with open drains. All drains are foreign bodies and therefore cause a tissue reaction, and should be used with care.

Monitoring infection

The infection control department should ideally audit wound infections and monitor the types of organisms harvested from wounds and chronic skin ulcers. Audit and surveillance are methods of assessing the effectiveness and efficiency of healthcare provision, and are now integral to health care delivery.

Most hospitals have guidelines for collecting information and analysis of nosocomial infection. Once the organisation's definition of wound infection is settled upon and accepted it is easy to count, assess and act upon. Most audit is based on process, in relation to outbreaks of infection, or outcome, which assesses the incidence of infection. The dissemination of data on wound infection rates to surgeons can lead to a decrease of infection without any other action. The identification of risk factors encourages the provision of extra support where it is needed; equally, rituals which are unrelated to wound infection may be questioned with obvious savings (for example, the use of masks or overshoes for all types of surgery). It has been suggested that clean wound infection rates are the most valuable reflection of surgical care in any hospital. However, follow-up of surgical wounds must be adequate to establish accurate infection rates. In these days of day-case and short-stay surgery, it must be remembered that most wound infections take 7–9 days to develop. Surveillance allows quality control, but anonymity of individual surgeons' infection rates should be respected and their use in 'league tables' is to be discouraged.

Preparation of the wound site

Pre-operative preparation of the skin is a contentious issue. The aim is to prevent postoperative wound infection, which has an incidence of 3.5–12.8%, depending upon the type of surgery performed (Cruse and Foord, 1980; Leigh, 1981; Mishinki, 1990). The traditional practice of pre-operative shaving has been reviewed (Freshwater, 1992); where patients are not shaved or are shaved in the theatre immediately before surgery, the clean wound infection rate is as low as 0.9%. Cruse and Foord (1973) recommended the avoidance of drains (especially open systems) and keeping operating time to a minimum to reduce incidence of postoperative wound infection.

The ease at which access to the operation site can be obtained depends on the organ undergoing surgery and its anatomical site. The surgeon, wherever possible, makes an incision directly over the site. Methods used to reduce tissue trauma during surgery include holding the scalpel at right-angles to the skin and incising or dissecting tissues in a way which minimises tissue shear and tension.

Following the procedure, wound closure is best achieved by approximating the wound edges immediately and accurately so that each tissue layer comes together, expediting haemostasis and the healing process.

Keyhole surgery

Since 1910 when laparoscopic surgery was first reported (Evantash and DeCherney, 1996), its use has become commonplace (Figure 7.3). Throughout the 1980s new instrumentation and videoscopy led to widespread use of laparoscopic surgery for many routine procedures such as tubal ligation and oophorectomy. Initially, the decrease in hospital stay, patient recovery time and potential for reducing postoperative morbidity encouraged the use of this technique as a cost-effective way of treating patients. However, it is not without its problems: reported complications include pneumoperitoneum-related problems, unrecognised haemorrhage, perforation injuries, infections, intestinal burns and cardiac arrest (Bailey, 1991). Critics argue that randomised controlled studies are needed before laparoscopic surgery is further developed (Evantash and DeCherney,

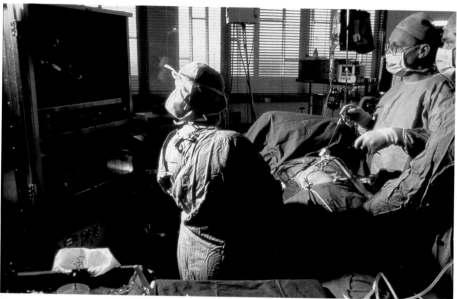

Figure 7.3 Keyhole surgery being performed

1996), whilst enthusiasts argue that the improved cosmesis, reduced hospital stay and recuperation time, early mobility and return to normal activity are beneficial.

Wound drainage

The use and history of drainage have been reviewed (Morison, 1992). Drainage systems are subdivided into active-suction and passive systems. There are a number of disadvantages of using drains, including:

- they act as retrograde conduits through which skin contaminants can gain access to deep layers of the wound
- they are essentially foreign bodies and, as such their presence reduces the tissues' resistance to infection
- they can cause pressure necrosis to internal organs and blood vessels, leading to the formation of fistulae or to secondary haemorrhage.

Dressings and postoperative care

Over the post 20 years there has been controversy over whether or not sutured wounds need dressing. Many surgeons use a simple, absorbent island dressing in theatre, which is removed 24 hours postoperatively. It has been recommended that it is not necessary to dress the wound further (Chrintz et al., 1989). However, with larger wounds where some further oozing may be expected, a semipermeable film dressing can be applied in theatre and left *in situ* until the sutures are removed (Bale and Jones, 1997). The advantages of using a film in this situation is that the patient can shower and the wound site can be observed as the dressing is transparent. In the postoperative period the wound site needs regular inspection, either daily, whenever the patient reports a change, or when there is an abnormality in observations.

Wound healing

The length of time sutures are left in situ depends on the wound site (and its blood supply) and the type of surgery performed. Wounds with an excellent blood supply include those on the head and neck. It is usual for sutures in this area to be removed at around three days. The abdomen may take 7–10 days to heal and the back up to 14 days.

Burns and scalds

These injuries are caused by excessive heat, which leads to degradation of protein and thrombosis of the capillaries resulting in tissue death. There are three main groups of burn injury: thermal, chemical and electrical.

Thermal burns

Fire, flames, hot fluids, steam, and direct contact with a hot surface are all examples of thermal injuries. The depth of tissue loss depends on both the intensity of the heat and the length of contact time (Figure 7.4). This type of injury is common in children, with around 2,500–3,000 being admitted to hospital in the UK with scalds and a similar number with burns each year (Forshaw, 1991) (Figure 7.5).

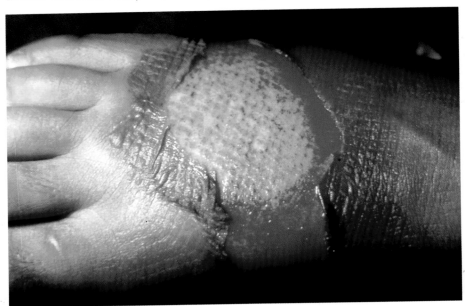

Figure 7.4 The depth of tissue loss in thermal injuries depends on the intensity of heat and the contact time

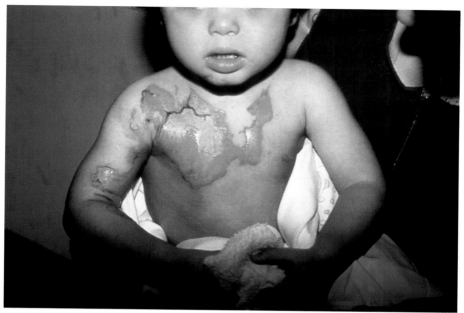
Figure 7.5 A thermal injury to a child caused by hot water

Legislation on nightwear has led to a dramatic reduction in the incidence of injuries related to burns caused by nightwear catching fire (Lawrence and Gowar, 1992). However changes in fashion related to the wearing of large T-shirts instead of fireguarded nightwear may cause some increase in such burns.

Incidence of some thermal injuries are increasing: kettle injury in children under five years of age is one such example, with kettle scalds very much increased over the past 20 years (Lawrence and Cason, 1994). A large epidemiological study from 1944 to 1993 describes the age and type of injury related to kettles (Lawrence and Cason, 1994). The reason for this increase is related to the use of electric jug kettles, where young children pull the electric cord and poor stability of the kettle results in injury. Across the whole spectrum of burns and scalds injuries, there is no evidence of a decrease in this type of injury (Lawrence, 1991). The Home Accident Surveillance System suggests that over 100,000 burns annually occur throughout England and Wales (Lawrence, 1991).

Chemical burns

Most chemical burns are industrial in nature and occur in the work environment (Herbert and Lawrence, 1989). These industrial burns are caused by the spillage of strong acids, alkalines and other corrosive chemicals (Dealey, 1994). The extent of the injury here depends on the nature of the chemical and the duration of contact with the skin. It may be 8–10 days before the full extent of the burn is apparent (Pannier, 1992), because alkaline and acid substances tend to be absorbed into the skin, resulting in progressive deepening of the injury. Where there is doubt about the chemical involved it is advisable to contact the manufacturer. Where the chemical make-up of a substance is unknown, it is advisable to use a neutral buffer solution to irrigate the injured area, as these are active against both alkaline and acidic chemicals. It is also important to remember that some chemicals can be absorbed through the skin into the circulatory system and tissues, and may have widespread toxic effects to major organs (Pannier, 1992).

Electrical burns

These burns are the result of an electrical current passing through the body. There will be both an entry and an exit site, and the extent of the internal damage may not be immediately apparent. The electrical resistance of the burnt tissue results in the release of heat, and the extent of the damage depends on the type and amount of current. An additional problem for patients sustaining electrical burns is that of cardiac arrhythmia; in-patient treatment is therefore recommended (Gowar and Lawrence, 1995).

Management

First aid A rapid response and appropriate care can reduce the depth of tissue damage. Copious irrigation or immersion in cold water will absorb heat and ease discomfort. Water should be applied before attempting to remove clothing, to save valuable time. Immersion should continue for at least 15, and up to 30 minutes.

Severe burns These injuries require fluid replacement, the amount depending on the surface area injured and the patient's age and body weight. The patient's haemodynamic condition should be monitored, with measurement of blood pressure and diuresis, which should be maintained above 40ml per hour. Following more severe burn injuries, fluid from the vascular sector diffuses into the interstitial sector, and the resultant oedema distends the tissues in and around the burn. Hypovolaemia can also occur where fluid is rapidly lost through the damaged skin. The brain, liver and kidneys can be affected by hypovolaemia, with rapid and permanent renal failure.

Assisted respiration This may be required for the more severely burned patient. Bronchoscopy using fibre optics may be required to check for primary bronchopulmonary damage following inhalation of toxic substances or hot gases.

Analgesia and sedation These are regularly used to relieve pain and distress, especially in the early days following injury, while control of body temperature is also necessary, as loss of skin alters body thermoregulation. Prevention of exudate evaporation, combined with controlling the temperature of the room, will help maintain body temperature.

Monitoring for pathogenic bacteria One of the main functions of the skin is to prevent the access of infection; when this barrier is broken the potential for invasion of pathogenic organisms is high. Septicaemia can account for more than 50% of burn-related mortality (Pannier, 1992).

Estimating the damage   It is traditional to describe a burn related to its depth, i.e. partial-thickness and full-thickness skin loss. The extent of the burn can be assessed by using Lund and Browder's (1944) chart (Figures 7.6a and 7.6b). This has been

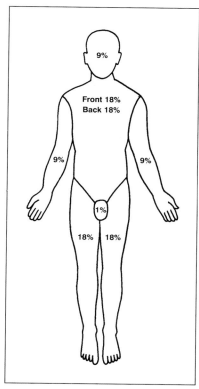

Figure 7.6a Estimation of surface area of burn — adults (Lund and Browder, 1944)

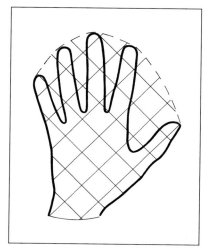

Figure 7.6b Surface area covered by patient's hand with fingers open = 1%

recommended as a more accurate method of assessing the extent of tissue damage than the 'Rule of Nine' (Wallace, 1951), as it takes account of the patient's age (Dealey, 1994).

Local treatment   Following cold water immersion, a temporary dressing is needed whilst the patient is taken to hospital. Household clingfilm and clean, wet compresses are excellent for this purpose (Gowar and Lawrence, 1995). All burns contain some dead tissue, removal of which is recommended together with other surface debris, including burnt clothing, to reduce the bacterial load on the injury. Gentle irrigation with water or physiological saline is recommended, although some antiseptics contain detergents that help to remove greasy contaminants (Gowar and Lawrence, 1995). Small scalds often require no dressings and can be left exposed as most skin erythema resolves within 48 hours. Where dressings are required a burns unit is likely to have its own preferred regimen, including the use of silver sulphadiazine creams, chlorhexidine tulles, 10% aqueous povidone iodine, film dressings and thin hydrocolloid films (Gowar and Lawrence, 1995).

Plastic surgery   At any stage in the management of the burns patient, plastic surgery may be considered. The range of options available to the plastic surgeon include:

- partial- or split-thickness skin grafts consist of the epidermis and some dermis
- pinch grafts are small pieces of skin laid onto the injury with spaces left in between
- full-thickness graft consists of epidermis and dermis
- skin flaps, myocutaneous rotation flaps, tissue expansion (Argenta, 1990); the use of these sophisticated techniques depends on the depth and site of the burn, the grafted area will need careful observation for failure or infection.

References

Al-Khateeb, T., Thomas, D.W., Shepherd, J.P. (1995) The management and repair of wounds of the face. *Journal of Wound Care* **4**: 8, 359–362.

Alexander-Williams, J., Oakes, G.D., Brown, P.P. et al. (1972) Abdominal wound infections and plastic wound guards. *British Medical Journal* (1973); **59**: 358–359.

Allen, D., Craig, E. (1994) The nervous system. In: Fawcett, J.N., Runciman, P.J. (eds) *Nursing Practice*. Edinburgh: Churchill Livingstone.

Argenta, L.C. (1990) Tissue expansion in forehead and scalp reconstruction. In: Staunch, B., Vasconez, L. (eds) *Grabb's Encyclopaedia of Flaps* (Vol. 1). Boston Ma: Little, Brown and Co.

Bailey, R.W. (1991) Complications of laparoscopic general surgery. In: Sucher, K.A. (ed.) *Surgical Laparoscopy*. St Louis Mo: Quality Medical Publishing.

Bale, S., Jones, V. (1997) *Wound Care Nursing: A patient-centred approach*. Hong Kong: Balliere Tindall.

Bartolo, D.C.C., Andrews, H., Virjee, J., Leaper, D.J. (1985) A comparative clinical and ultrasonic trial of a new Redivac drain after cholecystectomy. *Journal of the Royal College of Surgeons of Edinburgh*; **30**: 358–359.

Boenning, D.A., Fleisher, G.R., Campos, J.M. (1983) Dog bites in children: Epidemiology, microbiology and penicillin prophylactic therapy. *American Journal of Emergency Medicine* **88**: 17–21.

Central Statistical Office (1990) *Annual Abstract of Statistics*. London HMSO.

Chrintz, H., Vibits, H., Cordtaz, T.O. et al. (1989) Need for surgical wound dressings. *British Journal of Surgery* **76**: 204–205.

Cruse, P.J.E., Foord, R. (1973) A five-year prospective study of 23,649 surgical wounds. *Archives of Surgery* **107**: 206–271.

Cruse, P.J.E., Foord, R. (1980) The epidemiology of wound infection: A ten-year prospective study of 62,939 wounds. *Surgical Clinics of North America*; **60**: 27–40.

Dealey, C. (1994) *The Care of Wounds*. Oxford: Blackwell Scientific Publications.

Evantash, E.G., DeCherney, A.H. (1996) Laparotomy: Is there a difference? In: Sammarco, J., Stovall, T.G., Steege, J.F. (eds) *Gynaecologic Endoscopy: Principles and practices*. Baltimore Md: Williams and Wilkins.

Forshaw, A. (1993) Hydrocolloid dressings in paediatric wound care. *Journal of Wound Care* **2**: 3, 209.

Freshwater, D. (1992) Pre-operative preparation of the skin: a review of the literature. *Surgical Nurse* **5**: 5, 6–10.

Gowar, J.P., Lawrence, J.C. (1995) The incidence, causes and treatment of minor burns. *Journal of Wound Care* **4**: 2, 71–74.

Harland, R.N.L., Irving, M.H. (1988) Surgical drains. *Surgery*; **1**: 1360–1362.

Herbert, K., Lawrence, J.C. (1989) Chemical burns. *Burns* **15**: 381–384.

Holt, G.R. (1990) Concepts of soft-tissue trauma repair. *Facial Plastic Surgery* **23**: 1019–1030.

Jackson, D.W., Pollock, A.V., Tindall, D.S. (1971) The value of a plastic adhesive drape in the prevention of wound infection. *British Journal of Surgery* **58**: 340–342.

Lackmann, G.M., Graf, W., Isselstein, G., Tollner, U. (1992) Surgical treatment of facial dog bite injuries in children. *Journal of Cranomaxillofacial Surgery* **20**: 81–86.

Lawrence, J.C. (1991) The epidemiology of burns. In: *Proceedings of the 2nd European Conference on Advances in Wound Management*. London: Macmillan Magazines.

Lawrence, J.C. (1992) Burns and scalds associated with motor vehicles. In: *Proceedings of the 2nd European Conference on Advances in Wound Management*. London: Macmillan Magazines.

Lawrence, J.C., Cason, C. (1994) Kettle scalds. *Journal of Wound Care* **3**: 6, 289–292.

Lawrence, J.C., Gowar, J.P. (1992) Nightwear, fireguards and legislation. In: *Proceedings of the 2nd European Conference on Advances in Wound Management*. London: Macmillan Magazines.

Leigh, D.A. (1981) An eight-year study of postoperative wound infection in two district general hospitals. *Journal of Hospital Infection* **2**: 207–217.

Lewis, D., Leaper, D.J., Speller, D.C.E. (1984) Prevention of bacterial colonisation of wounds at operation: Comparison of iodine impregnated (Ioban) drapes with convential methods. *Journal of Hospital Infection* **59**: 142–146.

Lilley, H.A., Kombury, E.J.L., Wilkins, J.M.D. (1979) Limits to progressive reduction of resident skin bacteria by disinfection. *Journal of Clinical Pathology* **32**: 382–385.

Lund, C.C., Browder, N.C. (1944) Estimations of areas of burns. *Surgery, Gynaecology and Obstetrics* **79**: 352.

Mertz, P.M., Davis, S.C., Olivier-Gandia, M., Eaglstein, W.H. (1997) The wound environment: Implications from research studies for healing and infection. In: Krasner, D., Kane, D. (eds) *Chronic Wound Care* (2nd edn). Wayne Pa: Health Management Publications Inc.

Mishinki, S.F., Law, D.J.W., Jeffery, P.T. (1990) Factors affecting the incidence of postoperative wound infection. *Journal of Hospital Infection* **16**: 223–230.

Morison, M. (1992) *A Colour Guide to the Nursing Management of Wounds.* London: Wolfe.

Pannier, M. (1992) Burns and superficial acute wounds. In: Harting, K. (ed.) *Theory Advanced Wound Healing Resource.* Copenhagen: Coloplast

Wallace, A.B. (1951) The exposure treatment of burns. *Lancet* **1**: 501.

Seropian, R., Reynolds, B.M. (1971) Wound infections after pre-operative depilatory versus razor preparations. *American Journal of Surgery* **121**: 251–254.

Wishan, P.M., Huang, A. (1989) Pet-associated injuries: The trouble with children's best friend. *Children Today* **18**: 24–27.

8. Chronic wounds 1: Leg ulcers

Sue Bale and Keith Harding

The management of patients with chronic leg ulcers is a significant and costly healthcare problem in the UK. In 1985 a major survey of leg ulcer patients was undertaken in Scotland, and provided much basic demographic data on these patients (Callum et al., 1985). The study showed that leg ulceration is a common problem for elderly female patients (Box 8.1).

Estimates of the cost of treating patients in the UK with chronic venous ulceration varies: Lees and Lombert (1991) estimated around £600 million a year, while Morison and Moffatt (1994) suggested between £400 million and £800 million. The costs to patients in terms of pain and discomfort, social isolation and inconvenience cannot be calculated (Homer, 1994). As 99% of patients are cared for in the community (Callum et al., 1985) the burden of care falls on district nurses, nursing home staff, practice nurses and general practitioners (GPs).

Effective leg ulcer management requires a systematic four-stage approach:
- obtain an accurate diagnosis by history taking, examination and investigation
- design an appropriate management/treatment plan
- evaluate progress at regular intervals
- achieve a satisfactory patient outcome.

The diversity of conditions which may present with leg ulceration (Box 8.1), and the fact that any individual may be endowed with more than one aetiological factor (Box 8.2), make a structured and systematic approach to each individual essential. Only when the correct diagnosis has been made can the most appropriate treatment be given.

Clinical assessment

History

It is essential in addressing the problem of a chronically ulcerated leg to take an adequate history not only of the ulcer but of the patient as a whole; past illnesses and operations may

---

Box 8.1 Demographic data from Lothian and Forth Valley leg ulcer study (Callum et al., 1985)

Prevalence	**Age:Sex ratio** *(Male:Female)*	
10 per 1,000 in adult population	Under 65	1:1
36 per 1,000 in over 65s	65–75	1:2.6
	75–85	1:4.8
	85+	1:10.3

Box 8.1 Causes of leg ulceration

Vascular
Venous disease
- Deep venous occlusion
- Superficial valvular incompetence

Arterial disease
- Chronic peripheral vascular disease
- Hypertension – Martorell's ulcer
- Acute peripheral thrombosis/ embolism

Vasculitis
- Primary, acute leucocytoclastic/ mononuclear
- chronic granulomatous

Diabetes
- Diabetic distal vascular disease
- Neuropathy
- Hyperglycaemia
- Depressed leucocyte function

Other
- Blood disorders (e.g. sickle cell anaemia)
- Self-inflicted (factitious)

Neuropathy
- Systemic (multiple sclerosis)
- Local (spinal cord injury)

Systemic disease
- Rheumatoid arthritis
- Renal disease

Infection
- Local/systemic
- Bacterial/fungal/parasitic

Oedema
- Lymphoedema
- Congenital (Milroy's syndrome)/ acquired (groin surgery, malignancy)
- Congestive cardiac failure
- Dependency/immobility

Malignancy
- Primary skin lesion
- Marjolin's ulcer

Trauma
- Tissue loss
- Osteomyelitis

Box 8.2 Aetiology of leg ulcers (Browse and Burnard, 1982; Shami et al., 1992)

Causes of leg ulceration

• Venous disease	70%	• Vasculitis	2%
• Arterial disease	10–15%	• Trauma	2%
• Mixed disease	10–15%	• Miscellaneous	1%
• Diabetes	5%		

give vital clues as to the underlying cause of the ulcer (Figure 8.1). If, for example, the patient has previously had a colectomy for ulcerative colitis, a related cutaneous vasculitis

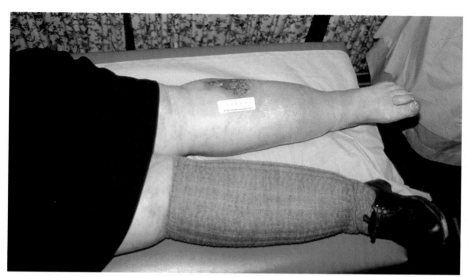

Figure 8.1 History-taking and examination are necessary to obtain an accurate diagnosis of causation

is a possibility. Patients may also be taking numerous prescribed drugs, some of which may have dermatological side-effects, or may interact with treatments such as antibiotics.

The history of the present episode of ulceration should include its duration, whether or not it is a recurrence of a previous lesion, and its current progress. Venous ulcers are often of long duration and are reported as recurrent in up to 66% of cases (Morison and Moffatt, 1994). Ischaemic ulcers, however, are more likely to be of recent onset. Symptoms associated with the ulcer may also give a clue about its aetiology. Pain is a characteristic feature of acute vasculitis, though any ulcer, if infected, may also be locally painful. This should not be confused with the pain of ischaemia which, though not related to the ulcer itself, usually affects the whole of the foot and lower leg. Obvious causative events such as trauma or a burn should also be sought.

Examination

Examination should start with the patient as a whole, looking for signs of systemic disease. Though not directly causative of leg ulceration, many factors may be contributing to poor wound healing which if treated appropriately would improve the chances of a successful outcome. Examination of the leg should extend from groin to the toes to ensure all factors that may influence healing are recognised. Ulcer size should be measured and documented so that the progress of treatment can be monitored.

Investigation

An important routine investigation which should be performed on every presenting patient is the measurement of the ankle and brachial systolic blood pressure and the calculation of the ankle/brachial pressure index (ABPI). This assesses the adequacy of the peripheral circulation, and whether any arterial disease is present: it is as important to know that arterial disease is absent as that it is present and may be causing the ulcer. The mainstay of treatment of the most common type of ulcer, the venous ulcer, involves compression therapy of some kind. However, application of compression in the presence of significant arterial disease can further impair the blood supply to the leg and lead to distal necrosis, occasionally precipitating leg amputation (Morison and Moffatt, 1994).

The technique of ABPI measurement is uncomplicated and easily learned by both doctors (Ray et al., 1994) and nurses (Cameron, 1991) after appropriate training. Using a hand-held Doppler (HHD) ultrasound machine, either the dorsalis pedis or posterior tibial artery is located. A sphygmomanometer cuff previously placed around the calf is then inflated to a level sufficient to abolish the Doppler signal. This is the systolic pressure in this artery. The same process is repeated with a brachial artery and the cuff around the upper arm. The pressure in the leg is then divided by the systolic pressure in the arm to give the ABPI. An index of 0.8 or greater suggests there is no significant arterial disease present. Diabetes and large amounts of puerpural oedema can make this test less accurate.

Photoplethysmography (PPG) is a useful test to identify venous disease and to differentiate between superficial and deep vein incompetence; it works by assessing the variations in light absorption of the skin by haemoglobin in the dermal venous plexus. A full dermal venous plexus and high venous pressure will absorb light. The transmission of light will increase as venous pressure decreases and the venous plexus empties. Additional tests used to determine venous insufficiency include strain-gauge plethysmography, light reflex rheography, foot volumetry and phlebography. Of late, duplex Doppler ultrasound has been used in the assessment of venous reflux and venous thrombosis. Disorders anywhere in the vascular tree, from the aortic valve of the heart, to the capillaries of the skin and the draining veins of a limb can cause ulceration; venous disorders account for the greatest proportion of leg ulcers.

Venous disease

Chronic venous insufficiency can be caused by thrombosis or varicosity damaging the valves in the veins of the leg. When the veins of the leg are damaged, blood can flow back towards the capillary bed, producing venous hypertension. Over time these capillaries become enlarged, distorted and increasingly permeable. Fibrinogen and red blood cells leak into the extra vascular space, haemoglobin is broken down resulting in haemosiderin staining of the skin. The skin is very fragile and even trivial injury can lead to the development of an ulcer (Figure 8.2). Lipodermatosclerosis and venous leg ulcers commonly occur around the gaiter area of the lower leg. The ulcers are superficial and often develop slowly, but can cover large areas of the lower leg and may become circumferential.

Pathophysiology

The primary function of the venous system in the lower extremity is the return of venous blood from the capillary network to the heart. Venous stasis resulting from poor venous return may have numerous causes, including congestive heart failure, low serum protein

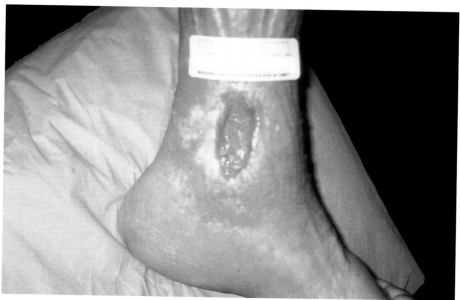

Figure 8.2 A typical venous leg ulcer

levels, pregnancy, obesity, post-phlebitic syndrome and incompetent valves leading to venous reflux. These conditions all tend to increase venous hydrostatic pressure, overcoming the osmotic pressure gradient and resulting in oedema.

Incompetent valves within the perforating veins connecting the superficial to the deep systems in the leg causes increased venous tension and an inability to reduce venous tension on exercise. With such sustained venous hypertension, blood is diverted from closed to open capillaries. There is a decrease in the number of capillary loops, but when damaged, these allow leakage of fibrinogen and subsequent fibrin barrier formation. This may lead to ulceration with associated induration and lipodermatosclerosis (Box 8.3).

Location and clinical features

The size and location of venous ulcers vary, yet they are most commonly found on the medial aspect of the leg. The long saphenous vein is the primary drainage channel of the medial ankle, and damage to it will result in ulceration. It is for this reason, that the medial ankle is a more common site of ulceration than either the lateral ankle or upper leg (Box 8.4).

Venous ulcers must be differentiated from other lesions of the lower extremity including lesions of diabetic, arterial, neuropathic and malignant aetiology. In addition, venous ulcers are often complicated by bacterial infection.

Using the history, examination and results of the appropriate investigations (Boxes 8.4–8.6), an accurate diagnosis of the aetiology of the ulcer can be made, and the main

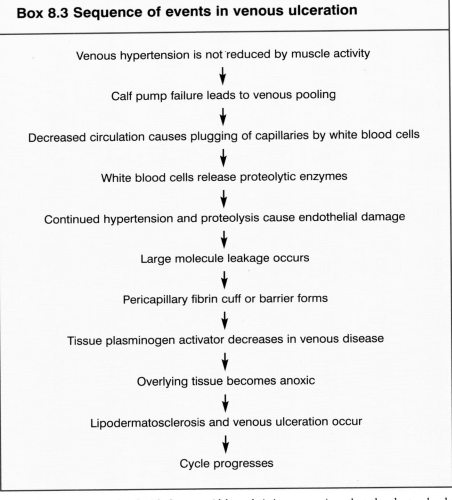

Box 8.3 Sequence of events in venous ulceration

Venous hypertension is not reduced by muscle activity

↓

Calf pump failure leads to venous pooling

↓

Decreased circulation causes plugging of capillaries by white blood cells

↓

White blood cells release proteolytic enzymes

↓

Continued hypertension and proteolysis cause endothelial damage

↓

Large molecule leakage occurs

↓

Pericapillary fibrin cuff or barrier forms

↓

Tissue plasminogen activator decreases in venous disease

↓

Overlying tissue becomes anoxic

↓

Lipodermatosclerosis and venous ulceration occur

↓

Cycle progresses

aims of treatment can be decided upon. Although it is appropriate that the doctor leads the team in obtaining a diagnosis, the treatment/management plan is usually best undertaken by the nurse, who is the healthcare professional involved in the day-to-day care of the patient and likely to provide the bandaging skills and wound care expertise.

Nursing intervention with venous ulcers

The patient is the most important person involved in a management plan; this statement may seem obvious, but the success or failure of treatment lies here. Using terms and phrases familiar to the individual, together with drawings where necessary, the patient should be given an explanation of the plans suggested. It is important that the patient

Box 8.4 Common clinical features of venous ulcers

- May be found in association with tortuous, engorged leg veins
- May, or may not be associated with trauma
- Painful when infected or desiccated
- Associated with periwound eczema
- Associated with lipodermatosclerosis
- Commonly located on the medial leg or ankle
- May be associated with a large amount of exudate
- Associated with prominent subcutaneous venules over the medial malleolus when the patient stands (ankle flare sign)
- Associate with eczema and hyperkeratosis
- Often accompanied by ankle oedema

Box 8.5 Local wound assessment

1. Document condition of the wound bed, i.e., dry, heavily exuding, healthy, sloughy/necrotic or infected
2. Trace around the circumference using an indelible ink marker to map out the wound onto a clean/sterile plastic sheet; these are available commercially
3. Measure the depth if appropriate

Box 8.6 Recording the ankle brachial pressure index (ABPI)

1. Make the patient comfortable on a bed or couch, lying as flat as possible
2. To obtain the brachial reading use a sphygmomanometer to record the systolic blood pressure at the brachial artery
3. To obtain the ankle reading of the affected limb, apply contact gel to the dorsum of the foot and move it around until you detect the dorsalis pedis pulse (when this is absent use the posterior tibial pulse). Inflate the cuff until the pulse is lost and slowly deflate until the pulse returns. This gives the systolic pressure reading
4. To calculate the ABPI, divide leg pressure by arm pressure
5. In the elderly repeat this measurement around every three months

understands why the ulcer has developed, and what the aims of their treatment are, in order to fully co-operate in the care plan, which might consist of:

- Define aims of treatment
- Select primary wound contact material
- Select bandaging system/compression hosiery (Figures 8.3–8.5)
- Refer for physiotherapy
- Evaluate treatment
- Give health promotion information.

Treatment aims

Ideally the aim of treatment for patients with venous ulcers is to achieve complete healing within an acceptable time frame. Patient co-operation is a major influencing factor, as compliance with compression bandaging, rest and exercise will affect the outcome.

Wound contact material Selection of an appropriate material will depend on the condition of the wound bed.

Bandaging/compression hosiery The aim is to provide around 40mmHg pressure at the ankle graduating to around 20mmHg at the knee (Box 8.7).

Physiotherapy This is aimed at exercising the calf muscle pump to assist the venous circulation, and elevating the leg for an hour during the day.

Evaluation of treatment This may initially be undertaken weekly to assess patient comfort and compliance, wound measurement and condition of the wound bed.

Health promotion Education to encourage weight loss where appropriate, exercise, rest and, when resting, elevation of the affected limb to reduce oedema.

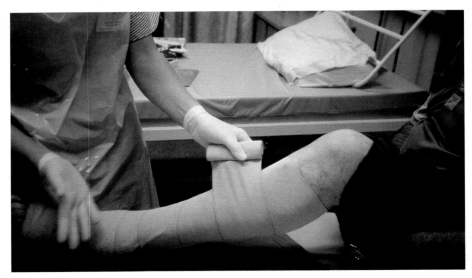

Figure 8.3 Applying compression bandages

Box 8.7 Bandaging systems (Thomas 1995; Morison and Moffatt 1994)

Extra high compression (Type 3d) (>50mmHg)
Elastic web bandage BP,
Elastoweb®, Tensopress®

High compression (Type 3c) (40mmHg)
Setopress®, Tensopress®

Moderate compression (Type 3b) (30mmHg)
Veinopress®

Light compression (Type 3a) (20mmHg at ankle)
K crêpe®, Litepress®, Tensolastic®

Multilayer system
K-four®, Profore®, Ultrafour®

Multilayer components
Layer 1 - Orthopaedic wool
Layer 2 - Retention crêpe
Layer 3 - A lightweight elastomeric
    bandage
Layer 4 - A cohesive bandage

Short-stretch bandages
Comprilan®

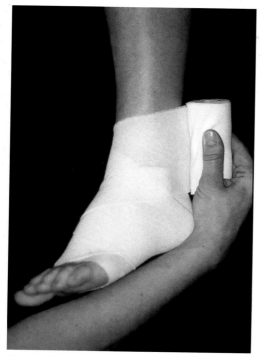

Figure 8.4 Applying short-stretch bandages

A systematic review of compression treatment for venous leg ulcers (Fletcher et al., 1997) estimated the effectiveness, in both clinical and cost terms, of compression systems. The authors searched 19 electronic databases, using the rate of healing and proportion of ulcers healed as the main outcome measure; 24 randomised controlled trials were identified. The results showed that the research evidence was quite weak due to inadequate sample size and poor methodology of the studies. However, compression did seem to increase healing rates and, in general, high-compression regimens were more effective than low. This review also concluded that there is insufficient evidence to indicate which system is the most effective.

Box 8.8 Classes of compression stockings

Class	Pressure
1	14–18mmHg at the ankle
2	18–24mmHg at the ankle
3	25–35mmHg at the ankle

Infection

Infection in an ulcer is often characterised by pain and increased exudate and odour. Most ulcers are colonised by skin commensals such as coagulase-negative staphylococci, non-haemolytic streptococci and coryneforms. This does not usually affect healing, though clinical infection with *Staphylococcus aureus* and particularly Group A streptococci can rapidly increase the size of the ulcer and lead to spreading cellulitis with systemic upset. If suspected, swabs can be taken from the ulcer bed and the patient treated with systemic antibiotics. Topical antibacterials may have a role in the management of ulcer infection but should not be used on a routine basis.

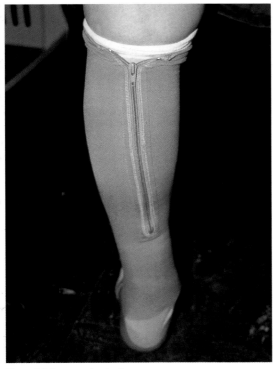

Figure 8.5 Compression hosiery

Arterial ulcers

The correct diagnosis of peripheral vascular occlusive disease in a patient presenting with a leg ulcer may save the patient's limb if not their life: 20–40% of patients with leg ulcers have some degree of arterial disease (Cornwall et al., 1986; Baker et al., 1992; Ruckley et al., 1982; Nelzen et al., 1991), and it is the primary cause of the ulcer in around 10% (Cornwall et al., 1986; Baker et al., 1992; Nelzen et al., 1991; Salaman and Harding, 1994).

A primary arterial ulcer is usually the result of severe vascular disease. The patient will usually have a history of gradually worsening symptoms over a period of time. Intermittent claudication should be sought in

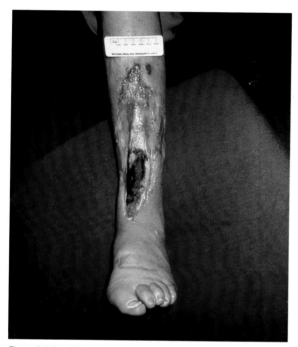

Figure 8.6 Arterial leg ulceration

the history: classically, pain occurs in the muscles of the leg after walking a specific distance; symptoms occur earlier if the patient is walking uphill or walking quickly. To satisfy the criteria for claudication however, the pain must resolve with rest and recur with continued exercise. Worsening of the occlusive disease shortens the claudication distance to a degree that it begins to interfere with normal activities. Eventually the foot may be so ischaemic that pain may occur at rest: this pain is usually located in the foot, as it is the most distal and therefore most poorly perfused part of the limb. Rest pain is characteristically worse at night when the leg is elevated. Patients will often admit to sleeping with the affected leg hanging out of the bed as this reduces their pain. They are in effect using gravity to increase the perfusion pressure of the leg and improve flow, thus reducing their symptoms. Patients should be asked about family history of vascular disease, and smoking history, as treatment of familial hyperlipidaemia and cessation of smoking are important in influencing the progress of arterial disease.

Ulcers due to arterial disease are most likely to be situated on the foot (Figure 8.6): 74% of ulcers below the ankle are due to arterial disease (Baker et al., 1992); often the tip of, or a whole toe becomes ulcerated. Ulcers may also develop as a result of minor trauma to the leg or over bony prominences. The nature of an ischaemic ulcer (Figure 8.7) means that it will be poorly vascularized. This results in necrosis and slough formation. The bed of the ulcer rarely develops granulation tissue, and tendon or even bone may be visible. The ischaemic leg will be cooler than the other with a poor capillary return and dry, hairless skin. For practical purposes, an ABPI of more than 0.8 is used as a cut-off to exclude arterial disease. With an ABPI of 0.7 one would expect a patient to have symptoms of intermittent claudication, though this level of ischaemia is rarely severe enough to cause ulceration alone. An ABPI of 0.4–0.5, however, denotes more severe disease. The patient may complain of rest pain and is at risk of spontaneous ulceration. Below 0.4 the limb can be regarded as critically ischaemic and may have altered sensation and skin necrosis. Referral for the advice of a vascular surgeon will ascertain whether angioplasty or reconstructive surgery is an option.

Nursing intervention with arterial ulcers

Treatment aims

Ideally, surgical intervention will be used to restore the damaged blood supply; however, this is not always feasible. Where arterial intervention is not indicated the aim of treatment is to maintain the affected limb and ulcer and to observe for deterioration.

Wound contact material Selection of the most comfortable dressing is appropriate here. Hydrogels can be effective in removing slough commonly associated with this type of ulcer.

Bandaging system This is to provide gentle support and retain the primary wound dressing. Compression is inappropriate in this situation and could further impair the poor blood supply.

Physiotherapy This has limited application, although gentle exercises can be useful in maintaining mobility in the ankle and knee joints.

Evaluation of treatment Because deterioration of the affected limb can occur so quickly, regular measurement of wound size and the condition of the wound bed is often necessary. Sepsis and rapid expansion of the ulcer can lead to amputation.

Health promotion/education Smoking can adversely affect the already poor blood supply. Smokers should be supported and encouraged to stop.

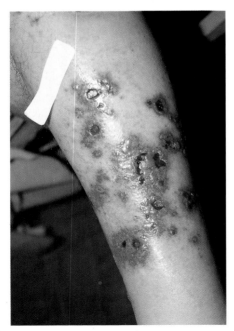

Figure 8.7 Vasculitic leg ulceration

Vasculitic ulcers

The reported incidence of vasculitis as a cause of leg ulceration is poorly documented. Only two studies included it as a primary cause, accounting for 2–4% of ulcers (Baker, 1992; Salaman and Harding, 1994). The vasculitides are a heterogeneous group of disorders whose only common link is that they cause focal inflammation of the walls of blood vessels. They can affect any vessel in the body and produce varied symptoms, dependent on the site and severity of inflammation. Groups of symptoms and signs commonly associated with each other have been collected together into a vast array of syndromes.

Vasculitic ulcers are usually on the shin and often appear clean, shallow and otherwise healthy, though slough and necrosis may be present in the acute phase. The ulcer may be surprisingly painful despite the absence of infection. The final diagnosis should be made by taking a biopsy for histological examination.

Management of vasculitic ulcers is difficult; a high proportion of lesions remain open despite prolonged treatment (Salaman, 1994). Systemic steroids can be of benefit, as can cytotoxic therapy (Fauci et al., 1979).

Malignant ulcers

Around 1% of leg ulcers are malignant (Figure 8.8). Patients with a history of long-standing ulceration (over five years) with or without local changes to the wound bed should be referred for medical assessment and possibly biopsy.

Mixed aetiology ulcers

Treatment aims

The combination of venous and arterial disease present in a limb makes effective treatment extremely difficult. However, where the degree of arterial disease is moderate (ABPI >0.8) the patient may be able to tolerate a light support bandage.

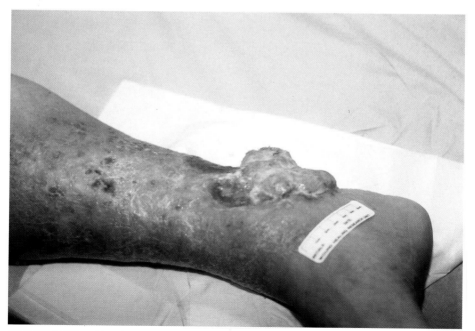

Figure 8.8 A malignant leg ulcer

Wound contact material Select the most appropriate.

Bandaging system Where the APBI is ≤0.8 apply no compression. Where the APBI >0.8 apply light support bandages.

Physiotherapy Walking and calf muscle pump exercises are extremely useful to aid venous return, and can be encouraged if and when arterial insufficiency allows.

Evaluation of treatment Progress towards healing is likely to be slow, as the blood supply is poor. Where steady progress is being maintained, monthly assessment is often sufficient.

Health promotion/education As for venous and arterial ulcers.

References

Baker, S.R., Stacey, M.C., Sing, G. et al. (1992) Aetiology of chronic leg ulcers. *European Journal of Vascular Surgery* **6**: 245–251.

Browse, N.L., Burnard, K.G. (1982) The cause of venous ulcerations. *Lancet* **ii**: 243–243.

Callum, M.J., Harper, D.R., Dale, J.J. et al. (1985) Arterial disease in chronic leg ulceration: An underestimated hazard? Lothian and Forth Valley Leg Ulcer Study. *British Medical Journal* **294**: 929–931.

Cameron, J. (1991) Using Doppler to diagnose leg ulcers. *Nursing Standard* **5**: 25–27.

Cornwall, J.V., Dore, C.J., Lewis, J.D. (1986) Leg ulcers: epidemiology and aetiology. *British Journal of Surgery* **73**: 693–696.

Fauci, A.S., Katz, P., Haynes, B.R. et al. (1979) Cyclophosphamide therapy of severe systemic necrosing vasculitis. *New England Journal of Medicine* **301**:235–238.

Fletcher, A., Cullum, N., Sheldon, T.A. (1997) A systematic review of compression treatment for venous leg ulcers. *British Medical Journal* **315**: 576–580.

Homer, C. (1994). Patients perceptions of chronic leg ulcers. *Journal of Wound Care* **3**: 2, 99–101.

Lees, T.A., Lambart, D. (1992) Prevalence of lower limb ulceration in an urban health district. *British Journal of Surgery* **92**: 1032–1034.

Morison, M., Moffatt, C. (1994) *A Colour Guide to the Assessment and Management of Leg Ulcers.* London: Mosby.

Nelzen, O., Bergqvist, D., Linghagen, A. (1991) Leg ulcer aetiology: A cross-sectional population study. *Journal of Vascular Surgery* **14**: 5457–5464.

Ray, S.A., Srodon, P.D., Taylor, R.S. et al. (1994) Reliability of ankle:brachial pressure index measurement by junior doctors. *British Journal of Surgery* **81**: 188–190.

Ruckley, C.V., Dale, J.J., Callam, M.J. et al. (1982) Causes of chronic leg ulcers. *Lancet* **2**: 615–616.

Salaman, R.A. What is vasculitis? (1994) *Proceedings Fourth European Conference on Advances in Wound Management.* London: Macmillan Magazines.

Salaman, R.A., Harding, K.G. (1994) *Aetiology and prognosis of chronic leg ulcers. Proceedings Fourth European Conference on Advances in Wound Management.* London: Macmillan Magazines.

Shami, S.K., Shields, J.G., Scurr, J.H., Coleridge Smith, P.D. (1992) Leg ulceration in venous disease. *Postgraduate Medical Journal* **68**: 779–785.

9. Chronic wounds 2: Diabetic foot ulcers and malignant wounds

Sue Bale and Keith Harding

Diabetic foot ulcers

Diabetes mellitus affects 1–2% of the population in the UK (Foster, 1997), and there are an estimated 750,000 people with diabetes in the UK (Williams, 1994). There is a rising trend in the incidence of diabetes, and the number of patients experiencing foot ulceration is therefore likely to increase. The problem of diabetic foot ulceration is uncommon before the age of 40 years; between the ages of 60–69 years, 6% of people with diabetes experience foot ulceration, and in those aged over 80 years this rises to 14% (Walters et al., 1992).

Boulton (1994) reports that diabetes causes around 30,000 partial or whole-limb amputations, with a further 45,000 diabetic patients experiencing active foot ulceration at any one time. The economic impact of diabetic foot ulceration and its associated morbidity is high. Boulton (1994) estimates that 29,000 hospital admissions a year result from diabetic foot problems, costing the NHS £23 million.

Diabetic foot ulceration presents in two forms, neuropathic (62%) and ischaemic (38%) (Edmonds, 1987); although these are two distinct pathologies, they can co-exist in the same limb. Estimations of the number of non-traumatic amputations associated with diabetes vary; Connor (1987) reported that diabetes caused 45% of all lower limb amputations carried out in the UK, while Waugh (1989) reported a lower rate of 23%.

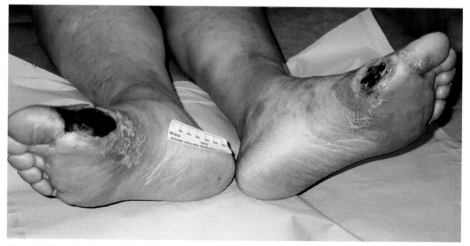

Figure 9.1 Neuro-ischaemic diabetic foot ulceration

Ulceration commonly precedes amputation, and the importance of preventing and healing diabetic foot ulcers is paramount. Infection further complicates ulceration; it has been suggested that it is the final common pathway leading to amputation of the foot (Pecoraro et al., 1991). It is estimated that 10–15% of all diabetic patients will develop ulcers on their feet and/or ankles at some time during their disease (Palumbo et al., 1985).

For healthcare professionals involved in the care of patients with diabetes, prevention and early treatment of foot ulceration are the keys to effective management of this patient group (Figure 9.2). Within Europe the St Vincent Declaration has set a target of reducing the amputation rate due to diabetic gangrene by 50%. The USA also set targets to reduce diabetic amputations by 40% by 2000 (Reiber, 1992). To achieve such targets the effective use of the diabetic foot care team is a key element (Connor, 1994; Edmonds et al., 1986). It is recommended (British Diabetic Association Working Party, 1990; Edmonds et al., 1986; Boulton and Connor, 1988) that diabetic patients have their feet checked regularly to prevent or detect the development of long-term foot pathologies, including ulceration and amputation. These foot checks can best be undertaken at a specialist foot clinic.

Further support for the use of foot clinics came in a recent evaluation of patient-held records; this reported that both the number of patients treated and the number referred have increased dramatically and also that amputation rates have fallen (Spencer and Widdows, 2000). Studies also report good success in terms of a reduction in hospital stays of 33% (Gibbons et al., 1993) and an 80% reduction in amputation rates (Assal et al., 1985) when foot ulcers are promptly treated, orthotic footwear is used, and a team approach taken with an ongoing education programme.

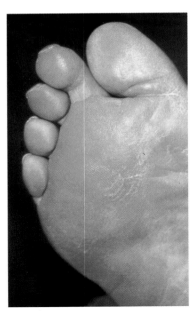

Figure 9.2 Ulcer-free foot in a diabetic patient

Aetiology and pathogenesis

A mixture of neuropathy and neuro-ischaemia account for 90% of diabetic foot ulceration, the remaining 10% having purely ischaemic disease (Boulton, 1996). In these conditions minor trauma to the foot causes ulceration, with infection of foot ulcers being a secondary complication. Sensory deficiency caused by diabetic neuropathy has been cited as the main cause of 'loss of protective sensation' (Cavanagh and Ulbrecht, 1994). Having lost this protective sensation, unperceived trauma such as a shoe rubbing or a puncture injury, pressure and/or shear cause ulceration. The pathogenesis of diabetic foot ulceration has been summarised in a flow diagram (Box 9.1).

Neuropathy and neuro-ischaemia

The exact cause of neuropathy remains unclear, though it is thought to be related to an excess of

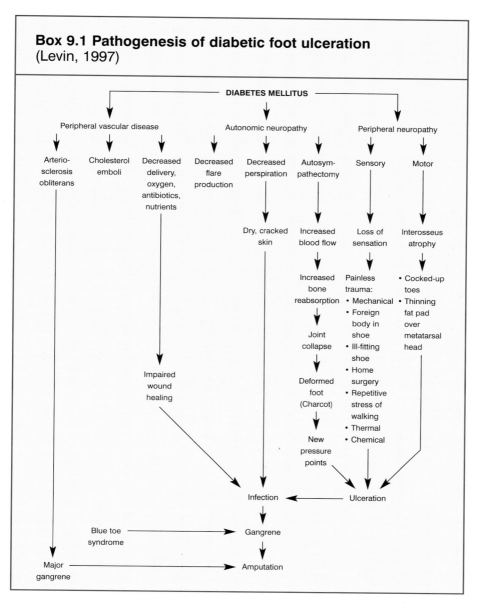

Box 9.1 Pathogenesis of diabetic foot ulceration (Levin, 1997)

sorbitol and fructose causing nerve damage (Watkins et al., 1997). There is, however, an opposing school of thought (Faber et al., 1993), which associates nerve damage with the depleted blood flow caused by microvascular disease. Here, poor blood supply to the vasa nervorum results in neural ischaemia and subsequent nerve damage. The type of neuropathy loss depends on the nerve type affected, sensory neuropathy being the most frequent but it is common for motor and autonomic neuropathy to also be present.

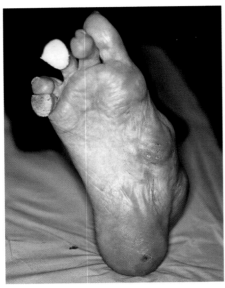

Figure 9.3 Charcot foot

Diabetic osteopathy (Charcot joint)

First described in 1868 by Charcot, this severe foot deformity is shown on X-ray as bony derangement, destruction and fractures (Knowles and Jackson, 1997; Dyer et al., 2000). In advanced Charcot foot disease the periarticular surfaces become completely resorbed and, attempts at healing of the bone give the characteristic 'wax running down a candle' appearance on an X-ray (Duet, 1994). The unstable joints in the Charcot's foot is described as 'a bag of bones' (Boulton, 1997), and as such is considered to be one of the most devastating morbidities associated with diabetes. The clinical signs of Charcot changes are erythema with a warm skin temperature but no generalised fever, and swelling without any obvious signs of ascending cellulitis (Figure 9.3).

Ischaemic ulcers

Although ischaemia alone accounts for only 10% of diabetic foot ulceration, critical ischaemia is associated with 62% of non-healing ulcers and is a causal factor in 46% of amputations (Gibbons, 1994). Macro and micro vessel disease has been discussed previously. Possible surgical interventions include sympathectomy, endarterectomy, angioplasty and bypass grafting (both proximal and distal). The increasing use of distal bypass surgery has been cited as reducing the length of hospital stays, reducing costs, maximising limb salvage and reducing the rate of amputation (Gibbons, 1994).

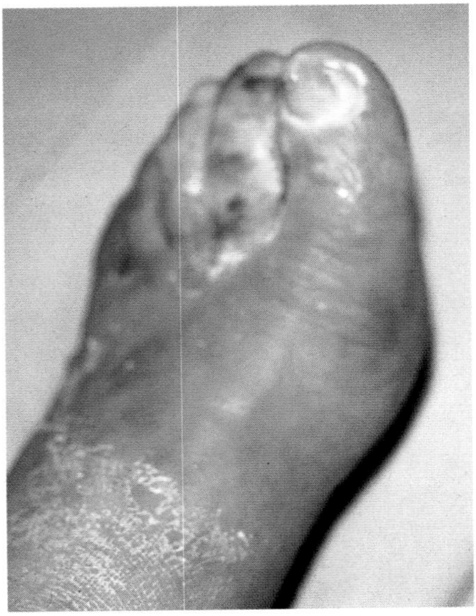

Infection

Infection is not a cause of but frequently occurs in the diabetic foot ulcer as a secondary complication (Figure 9.4). Infection worsens the prognosis for the limb and the majority of cases of gangrene are the direct result of severe infection. Here the arteriosclerotic blood vessels of the foot are occluded by thrombosis caused

Figure 9.4 Spreading infection

by infection of these blood vessels. Treatment options include:
- Regular foot inspection for early detection of clinical signs of infection
- Antibiotic therapy, bearing in mind that a wide range of organisms may be present; a bacteriological culture from a diabetic foot ulcer typically grows a mixture of Gram negative/positive and anaerobic organisms (Elkeles, and Wolfe, 1993). Treatment may be administered orally or intravenously and should continue for as long as the signs of infection persist.

Foot care

The role of health education

Effective health education has been recommended for the prevention and optimal treatment of diabetic foot ulceration (Fletcher and Jeffcote, 1994) (Box 9.2). Both patients and health professionals can benefit from education, though the advice given to patients needs to be both relevant and appropriate to their own priorities if behavioural change is to be achieved. Three target groups have been identified as benefiting from health education:

- Diabetic patients who are fit and healthy and whose feet are not at risk.

Education for this group consists of regular foot inspection, good foot hygiene, prompt treatment of fungal infections (e.g. athlete's foot), careful care of the toe nails to ensure that cutting these does not increase the risk of trauma or ingrowing toe nails. The importance of good foot care as the patient gets older needs to be emphasised, and techniques introduced gradually.

- Those whose feet are defined as being at particular risk because of neuropathy, neuro-ischaemia and/or other reasons, but who are otherwise fit and lead active lives.

Regular foot inspection together with the advice given to the first group is supplemented by foot assessment for pressure points and the observation of these areas:
- appropriate footwear prescribed by the orthotist service
- regular chiropody for nail care and the debridement of callus
- specific advice on avoiding traumatic injury, i.e. testing bathwater to avoid burns to the feet, sharp objects and cuts and grazes.

- Frail patients with at-risk feet, who are largely dependent on others. For many of these patients, poor mobility and poor eyesight make any of the above recommendations difficult to act upon themselves. Daily foot inspection by relatives and carers is recommended, together with orthotist and chiropody services.

The method of delivery of healthcare and education influences the likelihood of the advice being followed. Alienation of patients has been described, where education is delivered without regard for the group targeted (Fletcher and Jeffcote, 1994). Verbal advice can be supplemented with leaflets, booklets and videos; handouts which contain pictures and simple, easy-to-follow instructions may be of additional benefit.

Treatment

Debridement

The removal of callus and devitalised tissue is essential in the treatment of patients with neuropathic foot ulceration (Figure 9.5). The presence of devitalised tissue increases the risk of both wound infection and spreading infection. The presence of callus can lead to increased compression of the soft tissues and rupturing of capillaries. In addition, a build-up of old blood and ulcer fluids collects under callus and can lead to abscess and sinus formation deep in the tissues. By removing callus and devitalised tissues, sharp debridement can expose the ulcer and a healthy, viable wound bed. This procedure is usually undertaken by a chiropodist or podiatrist.

Using a scalpel the tissue is gradually pared away, layer by layer, until a healthy, bleeding bed is exposed. Sinuses and pockets can also be exposed in this way. Where there is a suspicion that deep tissue damage with bony involvement is present, a plain film X-ray may be requested to exclude osteomyelitis. As the ulcer heals, regular sharp debridement will be needed to prevent the callus from causing delay in cell migration or the growth of bacteria (McInnes, 1994). Patients with ischaemic disease warrant special caution, especially where infection is present.

Dressings

The use of a wide range of modern dressing materials has been described for the management of diabetic foot ulceration (McInnes, 1994). Providing that all other basic

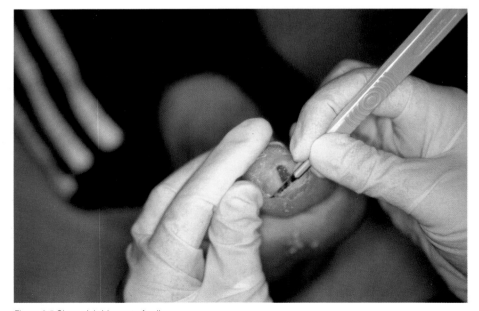

Figure 9.5 Sharp debridement of callus

Box 9.2 Daily foot care guidelines for people with diabetes (reproduced with kind permission of Smith and Nephew)

Foot care guidelines
- Wash feet daily using a soft cloth or cotton wool to clean between the toes
- Dry feet carefully with a soft towel, drying between toes thoroughly and gently
- Use moisturising cream daily on dry skin — avoid putting between toes unless advised otherwise
- Do not use corn or hard skin treatments, or anything else that may irritate the skin
- Inspect feet daily, using a mirror to check underneath; seek advice if skin becomes red, itchy, sore or cracked, or if open wounds appear
- Keep feet warm in winter with thick socks and thick-soled shoes
- Avoid sitting too close to fires and heaters, or putting the feet on hot sand, hot water bottles etc
- Cut nails following the shape of the toe; do not cut down corners or sides. If cutting toe nails is difficult, contact a podiatrist
- Change socks or tights daily; choose pairs with smooth seams which will not rub the toes
- Have feet measured every time new shoes are bought; choose soft leather and rounded toes, free from bulky seams
- Check inside shoes daily before wearing, to ensure no objects have got inside
- Do not walk barefoot, even in the house

Signs of infection
- Difficulty walking and/or applying shoes
- Swelling in part or all of the foot
- Redness or other discolouration
- The foot becomes hotter than normal
- Discharge or unusual odour
- Open sores or blisters
- Nausea, vomiting and high temperature
- Difficulty maintaining blood glucose control

care has been considered, the appropriate dressing material can be selected. It is important to note that the dressing material selected will probably be used in conjunction with specialised footwear or other orthotic devices. The dressing should not interfere with the functioning of such devices.

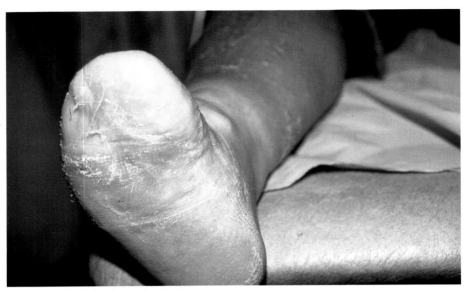

Figure 9.6 A diabetic foot that has had the toes amputated

Orthotic shoes

The provision of appropriate footwear for patients with neuropathic disease has been recognised as one of the most important aspects of their management (Tyrrell, 1995). Removal or reduction of damaging forces in order to protect the surrounding tissue forms a major part of treatment. There are three major forces operating on the foot which contribute to delayed healing and further ulcer development:

- Friction
- Compression (vertical pressure)
- Shear stress (Baker, 1997).

Footwear must be able to manage diminished sensation, toe deformities and prominent metatarsal heads, as well as ulcerated areas and callus build-up from pressure points. For patients who have undergone an amputation of the toes (Figure 9.6), orthotic shoes and off-weighting devices are essential to prevent further tissue destruction. In constructing a shoe the following features are considered:

- The shoe shape must hold the foot back in the shoe by using a strap or lace
- There must be room to allow extension of the forefoot without squashing the toes
- The shoe must provide sufficient length, width and girth for the shape and size of the foot
- Shoes must be balanced so that the height of the heel is matched with the toe spring
- Biomechanics of the foot may be assessed using specialised equipment; this will help in the construction of a shoe which provides support and cushioning for the distorted foot
- Last, but by no means least, the appearance and look of the shoe must be acceptable to the patient (Tyrrell, 1995).

Off-weighting

Although it is recognised that bed rest is the only way of ensuring complete removal of pressure from the foot, this can be an impractical method of managing the many thousands of patients who experience diabetic foot ulceration. Total contact casts were designed in 1983 and are applied with minimal padding to fit the lower leg like a glove. Vertical forces are evenly distributed over the sole of the foot, and shear forces are reduced so improving the chances of healing (Laing et al., 1991). Caution is required where infection is an issue, as this system makes observation and monitoring difficult. A range of casts is available for off-weighting pressure.

Scotchcast boots were developed to redistribute weight onto the foot while causing minimal interference with the patient's lifestyle. They provide weight redistribution and are a useful alternative to total contact casts. Dressing changes are possible with this system, although again great vigilance is required to detect any clinical signs of infection.

Total contact casts have been described as very efficient at redistributing pressure on the plantar area of the foot (Edmonds and Foster, 2000). Their application is an extremely skilled procedure, requiring training and experience to apply safely. Patients, their relatives and healthcare professionals need to be aware of the potential risks associated with totally enclosing the insensate foot in a cast. The cast needs to be removed and reapplied every week, at which time a full assessment of the foot and ulcer is undertaken.

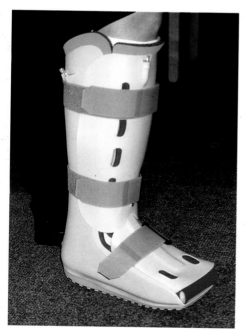

Figure 9.7 An Aircast walking brace

Aircast walking braces are removable systems that address many of the practical problems encountered by total-contact casting. The Aircast is a bivalved cast held together by Velcro strapping. The device has four air cells that can be inflated with a hand pump. Caution has been recommended in patients who have difficulty complying with casting, as this device can be easily removed.

The multidisciplinary team

The role of the multidisciplinary team is crucial to both the prevention and management of diabetic foot ulceration (Edmunds et al., 1986). These patients require the co-ordinated efforts of staff from a number of disciplines working together effectively as a team (Figure 9.8).

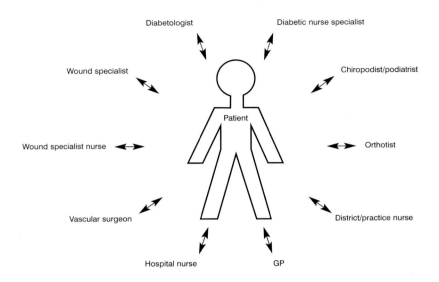

Figure 9.8 The multidisciplinary team involved in diabetic care

All members of the diabetic foot care team should be conveying the same message, and the information given must be appropriate and relevant to that individual. Audit of the service will help to ensure that an appropriate and acceptable standard of care is being delivered (Connor, 1994).

Social/psychological support

Chronic lower limb ulceration of whatever cause is a miserable condition which affects mainly elderly female patients. Many elderly females outlive their partners and so live alone, possibly on fixed incomes with little social contact. While treating the patient's leg ulcer it may be possible to improve social support. This can be achieved through luncheon clubs or day centres, and may have the added benefit of improving mobility and the patient's overall quality of life.

Malignant wounds

Of the three major groups of cancers, carcinomas and sarcomas are the most likely to produce ulceration and fungation in the latter stages of the disease. The most common type of fungating lesion is found in the female suffering from breast cancer, though malignancies of the skin, vulva and groin are not rare. A malignant ulcer has been defined as 'a break in epidermal integrity because of infiltration by malignant cells. This may be due to primary skin malignancy, metastatic deposits or extension of malignancy structures' (Saunders and Regnard, 1995). The process of fungation has been described as a mixture of concurrent and progressive disease which affects haemostasis, lymph, interstitial and cellular environments

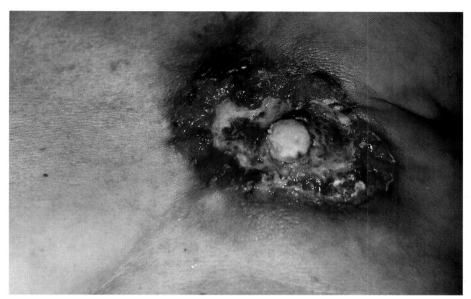

Figure 9.9 A fungating lesion of the breast

(Bridel-Nixon, 1997). As it enlarges, vascular distortion within the tumour causes areas of hypoxia, leading to tissue death (Grocott, 1993a). This devitalised tissue gives rise to the commonly associated anaerobic malodour. Other local wound problems include increased exudate production, asymmetry, bleeding or the fear of bleeding and pain.

Wound care

Often the prognosis for achieving healing is extremely poor. All treatments are aimed at symptom control and palliation, trying to improve the patient's quality of life. A patient-led approach has been recommended (Grocott, 1993b), in which patients are encouraged to identify their main problems, and subsequent treatment interventions are decided through the partnership of the clinician and patient.

In managing fungating wounds, knowledge of the range of dressings available, the use of topical antimicrobials and antibiotics, systemic antibiotics and odour-absorbing materials are required, as these are the traditional methods used to control symptoms. Combinations of products, although not generally recommended, can be invaluable in the management of difficult, fungating wounds (Banks and Jones, 1993). Newer developments have been described as more effective in managing fungating wounds on the head, neck and trunk. In particular the use of a foam latex mould has been described, which helps to keep dressings and padding in place (Grocott, 1993c).

The use of radiotherapy can, where appropriate, decrease both tumour bulk and exudate levels and also help ease pain. Referral to an oncologist for this type of treatment should be considered as a palliative treatment.

Surgical intervention

For some patients, surgical methods of treating fungating wounds may be appropriate, particularly where the wound is deteriorating and symptoms are becoming difficult to manage. Fungating breast tumours, for example, can be excised and covered by a myocutaneous rotation flap (Mortimer, 1993), completely resolving unpleasant wound symptoms for several months.

Clinical challenges

The clinical challenges in caring for a patient with a fungating tumour are in part similar to those required to manage other aetiologies (Box 9.3, Saunders and Reynard, 1995). Additional considerations include:

- Malodour
- Excess, sticky exudate
- Soiling of clothing
- Physical distress
- Psychological distress
- Very large, poor wound shape or location of the tumour (Grocott, 1993).

Additional therapies not included in Box 9.3 include:

- Use of a foam latex mould with a keyhole for access to the wound (Grocott, 1992)
- Use of bandages and tubular net garments for retaining dressings in contact with the wound where skin stripping from surgical tape could be a problem (Dealey, 1994)
- use of the full multidisciplinary palliative care team (Rubens, 1989).

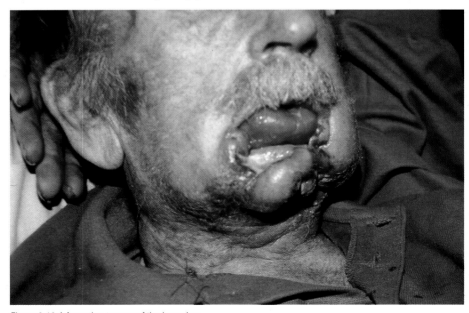

Figure 9.10 A fungating tumour of the lower jaw

Box 9.3 A flow diagram for malignant ulcers

(Saunders and Reynard, 1995; reproduced with kind permission of Edward Arnold)

Is ulcer bleeding? — YES →
- See flow diagram on bleeding (Reynard and Hockley, 1995)
- Consider radiotherapy or embolisation

NO ↓

Is an altered body image present? — YES →
- **Improve cosmetic appearance**: cosmetic camouflage, disguise cavities with foam or latex dressing, adapted breast prosthetics
- **Enable to cope with altered image**: acknowledge distress/explore issues (including sexual aspects)/refer for counselling if necessary

NO ↓

Is an altered body image present? — YES → **Will prognosis allow time for cleaning?** — YES →
- **Debride/deslough** gently with polysaccharide, hydrocolloid or hydrogel dressing. Do not use chlorine-releasing solutions (e.g. Eusol, Milton).

YES →
- **Treat odour**: topical 1% metronidazole gel
- **Mask odour**: charcoal cloth dressings (e.g. Actisorb, Cliniflex odour control dressing, Lyofoam C) or oxychlorodene (Ostobon) between dressings (not directly on tissues). Cling film (food wrap) can be used to cover dressing providing extra masking.

NO ↓

Is discharge excessive? — YES → **Is this a sinus or fistula?** — YES →
- **Reduce volume of discharge**:
  - **if adhesion on flat surface is possible**: paediatric aloma bag
  - **inflammatory**: topical steroids
  - **secretory**: topical hydrocortisone hydrobromide
  - **urine or faeces**: diversion, e.g. colostomy

NO →
- **Reduce inflammation**: topical high dose steroid (e.g. Dermovats) once daily for one week. Consider NSAID or systemic corticosteroids.
- **Absorb discharge**: high absorbency dressings e.g. hydrocellular Allevyn, alginate Kaltostat
- **Protect surrounding skin**: barrier ointment e.g. zinc ointment

NO ↓

Is pain present? — YES →
- **If only at dressing changes**:
  - alternative dressing technique
  - extra analgesia: additional dose of current analgesic 1 hour before change (not controlled-release morphine)/oxygen + nitrous oxide (Entonox) during change/topical local anaesthetic gel
- **Review systemic analgesia**
- **Consider**:
  - subcutaneous infusion of kelamine (1–10 mg/kg/24 hours)
  - spinal analgesia

NO ↓

Is ulcer itchy? — YES →
- **Remove allergen**: check for allergy to dressing or topical agent
- **Reduce inflammation**: consider NSAID drug or topical steroids.

NO ↓

Return to beginning

115

References

Assal, J.P., Muhlauser, I., Pernat, A. et al. (1985) Patient education as the basis for diabetes care in clinical practices. *Diabetologia* **28**: 602–613.

Baker, N.R. (1997) *Foot ulcer management. Journal of Wound Care Resource File.* London: Emap Healthcare.

Boulton, A.J.M., Connor, H. (1988) The Diabetic Foot. *Diabetic Medicine* **5**: 796–798.

Boulton, A.J.M. (1996) The diabetic foot. *Surgery* **14**: 2, 37–39.

Boulton, A.J.M. (1997) Foot problems in patients with diabetes mellitus. In: *Textbook of Diabetes* Volume 2. Oxford: Blackwell Scientific.

Bridel-Nixon, J. (1997) Other chronic wounds. In: Morison, M., Moffatt, C., Bridel-Nixon, J. et al. (eds) *A Colour Guide to the Nursing Management of Chronic Wounds.* London: Mosby.

British Diabetic Association Working Party (1990) *Diabetes and Chiropodial Care.* London: British Diabetic Association.

Cameron, J. (1991) Using Doppler to diagnose leg ulcers. *Nursing Standard* **5**: 25–27.

Cavanagh, P.R., Ulbrecht, J.S. (1994) Biomechanical aspects of foot problems in diabetes. In: Boulton, A.J.M., Connor, H., Cavanagh, P.R. (eds). *The Foot in Diabetes.* London: John Wiley and Sons.

Connor, J. (1987) *The Foot in Diabetes.* Chichester: Wiley and Sons.

Connor, H. (1994) Prevention of diabetic foot problems: identification and the team approach. In: Boulton, A.J.M., Connor, H., Cavanagh, P.R. (eds). *The Foot in Diabetes.* London: John Wiley and Sons Ltd.

Dyer, J.F., Ettles, D.F., Nichol, A.A. 92000) The role of radiology in the assessment and treatment of the diabetic foot. In Boulton, A.J.M., Connor, H., Cavanagh, P.R. (eds) *The Foot in Diabetes* (3rd ed.). Chichester: John Wiley and Sons Ltd.

Edmonds, M.E., Blundell, M.P., Morris, M.E. et al. (1986) Improved survival of diabetic feet: The role of the specialist foot clinic. *Quarterly Journal of Medicine* **60**(232): 763–771.

Edmonds, M.E. (1987) Experience in a multi-disciplinary diabetic foot clinic. In: Connor, H., Boulton, A.J.H., Ward, J.D. (eds) *The foot in diabetes.* Chichester: John Wiley & Sons.

Edmonds, M.E., Foster, A.V.M. (2000) *Managing the Diabetic Foot.* Oxford: Blackwell Scientific.

Elkeles, R.S., Wolfe, J.H.N. 91993) The diabetic foot. ABC of vascular disease. *British Medical Journal* **303**: 1053–1055.

Faber, W.R., Michels, P.P.J., Maats, B. (1993) The Neuropathic Foot. In: Westerhot (ed) *Leg Ulcers: Diagnosis and treatment.* Amsterdam: Elsevier.

Fletcher, E.M., Jeffcote, W.J. (1994) Footcare education and the diabetes specialist nurse. In Boulton, A.J.M., Connor, H., Cavanagh, P.R. (eds) *The Foot in Diabetes* (2nd ed.). Chichester: John Wiley and Sons Ltd.

Foster, A. (1997) Multidisciplinary care of the diabetic foot. *Journal of Wound Care Resource File.* London: Macmillan Magazines.

Gibbons, G.W., Maraccio, E.J., Burgess, A.M. et al. (1993) Improved quality of diabetic foot care, 1984 vs. 1990: Reduced length of stay and costs, insufficient reimbursement. *Arch Surg* **128**: 576–581.

Knowles, E.A., Jackson, N.J. (1997) Care of the diabetic foot. *Journal of Wound Care* **6**: 5, 227–230.

Laing, P.W., Cogley, D.I., Klenerman, L. (1991) Neuropathic foot ulceration treated by total contact casts. *Journal of Bone and Joint Surgery* **74-B**: 1, 133–136.

Levin, M. (1997) Diabetic Foot Wounds: Pathogenesis and management. *Advances in Wound Care* **10**:2, 24–30.

McInnes, A.D. (1994) The role of the chiropodist. In Boulton, A.J.M., Connor, H., Cavanagh, P.R. (eds) *The Foot in Diabetes* (2nd ed.). Chichester: John Wiley and Sons Ltd.

Palumbo, P.J., Melton, L.J. (1985) Peripheral vascular disease and diabetes. In: Harris, M.I., Hamman, R.F. (eds) *Diabetes in America* **85**: 1468, 1–21. Bethesda: National Institute of Health.

Pecoraro, R.E., Ahroni, J.H., Boyko E.J. et al. (1991) Chronology and determinants of lower-extremity ulcers. *Diabetes* **40**: 1304–1313.

Reiber, G.E., Pecoraro, R.E., Koepsell, T.D. (1992) Risk factors for amputation in patients with diabetes mellitus. A case control study. *Ann Intern Med* **117**: 95–105.

Reynard, C., Hockley, J. (1995) *Flow Diagrams in Advanced Cancer and Other Diseases.* London: Edward Arnold.

Salaman, R.A. What is vasculitis? (1994) *Proceedings Fourth European Conference on Advances in Wound Management.* Copenhagen: Macmillan Magazines Ltd.

Saunders, J., Reynard, C. (1995) Malignant Ulcers. In: Reynard, C., Hockley, J. *Flow Diagrams in Advanced Cancer and Other Diseases.* London: Edward Arnold.

Spencer, J., Widdows, C. (2000) Implentation of patient-held records in diabetic foot care. *Journal of Wound Care* **9**:2, 64–66.

Tyrrell, W. (1995) Shoes for people with diabetes. *Journal of Wound Care* **4**: 3, 123–126.

Walters, D.P. Gatling, W., Mullee, M.A. et al. (1992) The distribution and severity of diabetic foot disease: A community study with comparison to a non-diabetic group. *Diabetic Medicine* **9**: 354–358.

Watkins, P.J., Drury, P.L., Howell, S.L. (1997) *Diabetes and its management.* Oxford: Blackwell Scientific Publications. 218–238.

Waugh, N.R. (1989) Amputations in diabetic patients: A review of rates, relative risks and resource use. *Community Medicine* **10**: 279–288.

Williams, D.D.R. (1994) The size of the problem: Epidemiological and economic aspcts of feet problems in diabetes. In: Boulton, A.J.M., Connor, H., Cavanagh, P.R. (eds) *The Foot in Diabetes* (2nd ed.) Chichester: John Wiley.

10. Chronic wounds 3: Pressure ulcers

Sue Bale and Keith Harding

Historical evidence suggests that the development of pressure ulcers in the sick and elderly is as old as humanity. An Egyptian mummy has been found with pressure ulcers, which were treated with an animal skin graft (Thompson Rawling, 1961). To date, the oldest known publication reporting pressure ulcers was published by Fabricius (1593), although the connection with pressure had not been made at this time and the tissue injury was reported as 'gangraena'. From 1722 a number of European investigators described pressure ulcers as being caused by external pressure and related this to being bedbound, hence the term 'decubitus' (Schut, 1992). Dr Jean-Martin Charcot, possibly the most eminent neurologist of his day, suggested that pressure ulcers in patients with spinal injuries were due to a damaged nervous system and so were not preventable (Charcot, 1879). Over time this theory has been challenged; Florence Nightingale (1861) proposed that good nursing care could prevent pressure ulcers. It is interesting how this statement has been interpreted in the nursing world. Over time, the belief that good nursing care can prevent pressure ulcers has been superseded by the belief that bad nursing care causes them (Dealey, 1997).

For today's nurses, the challenge is to identify those patients at greatest risk of developing tissue damage, and then in providing the most appropriate interventions. There is much controversy surrounding the efficacy of interventions, and little solid evidence on which to base decisions as to the most effective care.

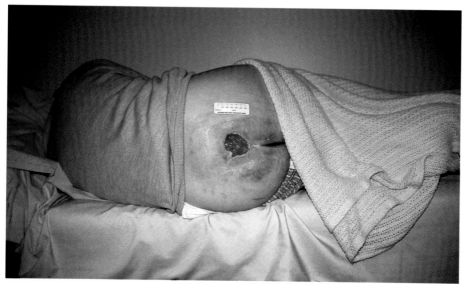

Figure 10.1 Extensive pressure damage in an elderly patient

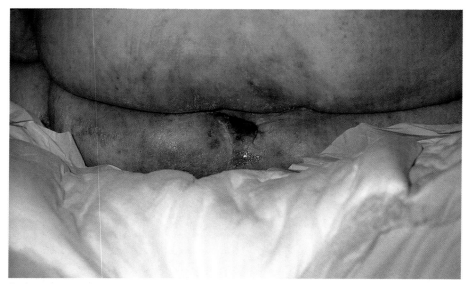

Figure 10.2 A pressure ulcer in an elderly patient following hospitalisation

Epidemiology

Pressure ulcers are most commonly associated with older people and the chronically sick and disabled (Figures 10.1 and 10.2). Within the UK, the numbers of elderly are rising within the population, with most of this growth in the over-85 age group (Bale and Jones, 1997). In the UK, by the year 2031 the proportion of the population over the age of 65 is expected to rise from 16% to 20.5% (OHE, 1992). It is recognised that the elderly suffer from more pathologies than younger individuals (David et al., 1983). With the increasingly elderly population the number of complex cases of pressure ulceration will increase.

Prevalence and incidence rates

Pressure ulcer prevalence and incidence rates are used to determine the extent of the pressure ulcer problem. This information is useful for evaluating the effectiveness of interventions and in the planning of resource use and allocation.

The pressure ulcer prevalence rate is the total number of patients with pressure ulcers occurring at a given time in a certain population. It is expressed per 1000 population.

The pressure ulcer incidence rate is the number of of new patients with pressure ulcers in a population in a given period of time. This is usually expressed per 1000 population per year.

In general, prevalence surveys are easier to carry out than incidence surveys, though prevalence surveys only provide a 'snapshot' picture of the problem. Dealey (1997) reviewed both prevalence and incidence surveys published after 1980, and reported that prevalence rates appeared to be increasing. She speculated whether this was due to an actual increase in numbers or an increased awareness among nurses of tissue damage.

Statistical data on a range of diseases (such as heart disease and cancer) are collected systematically and centrally, enabling society to estimate the costs associated with the rise and fall in incidence and prevalence of such disease. However, in the UK, no such systematic data collection is undertaken for patients who develop pressure ulcers. Numerous estimates of incidence, prevalence and cost have been calculated in an attempt to define the extent and cost of this problem (Bridel-Nixon, 1997; Dealey, 1997). These estimates are based on local data from individual hospitals and trusts, and extrapolated into the whole country. Incidence ranges from 3.4% to 43% and prevalence from 4% to 18.6% in hospitalised patients. In the community an overall prevalence of 4.4% has been reported (Hallett, 1996), with a range from 0% in learning disabilities settings to 18.6% in an elderly acute unit. Within the very different healthcare system of the USA, pressure ulcer prevention is tackled at a national level. The Agency for Health Care Policy and Research (AHCPR) supported the development and implementation of national guidelines for the prediction and prevention of pressure ulcers in adults (NPUAP, 1992). An expert panel employed an explicit methodology and expert clinical judgement in producing the guidelines. The literature search included around 800 manuscripts and sought advice and opinion from a broad range of individuals and organisations. These guidelines are widely and freely available and are supported by many professional organisations including the National Pressure Ulcer Advisory Panel (NPUAP). In Europe, the European Pressure Ulcer Advisory Panel (EPUAP) was established in 1996 and functions in a similar manner to the NPUAP in producing guidelines and the widespread dissemination of information.

Pathogenesis and pathophysiology

Although most tissue damage occurs in the skin, the deep fascia, muscle and bones can also be involved in more extensive damage. The skin is the largest organ in the body and receives about a third of its blood supply. The main functions of the skin are to:

- Provide a waterproof but water vapour- and gas-permeable covering; it is a protective covering against mechanical damage
- Manufacture vitamin D
- Store fat
- Regulate temperature
- Act as a major sensory organ.

There are three layers of the skin (Figure 10.3), the epidermis, the dermis and the hypodermis (subcutaneous tissue).

The epidermis This is the avascular, outer layer of the skin. It consists of dead keratinised cells which are arranged parallel to the surface of the body, being derived from the proliferating basal cell layer of the epidermis adjacent to the dermis. The epidermis is thickest on the soles of the feet and palm of the hand. It forms a physical barrier against water, bacteria and chemicals.

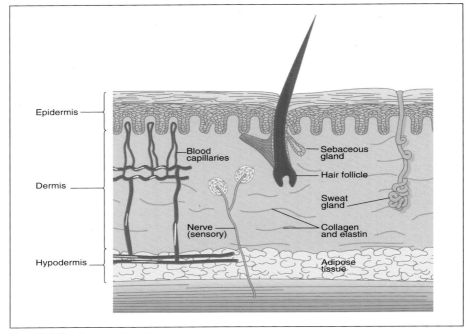

Figure 10.3 The structure of the skin

The dermis This is highly vascular and well supplied with sensory receptors to pain, temperature and touch. It also contains blood capillaries, sebaceous glands, sweat glands, hair follicles and lymphatic capillaries. These structures are contained by a matrix of collagen and elastin.

The hypodermis This consists of adipose and loose connective tissue that provides a fat store and also has the ability to absorb energy.

The skin is a viscoelastic structure with a viscous component (due to its fluid content) and an elastic component (due to elastin fibres which are interwoven with collagen) (Scales, 1990). Where external pressure is applied the collagen fibres rotate until they are aligned; as external pressure is released the associated elastic fibres restore the tissue. This response to direct pressure is an important function of the collagen/elastin matrix (Bridel, 1993). With advancing age the amount of collagen and elastin in the skin decreases, so reducing its ability to absorb direct pressure.

The deep fascia underlies adipose tissue as an avascular and inelastic membrane covering muscles (Bridel, 1993). In health, an unimpaired blood supply delivers vital oxygen and nutrients to the skin, while normal sensation during both sleep and the waking day ensures regular repositioning. However, in ill-health a number of factors can alone, or in combination, lead to tissue death and the development of a pressure ulcer. The type and duration of the pressure exerted further complicate this and the effects vary depending on the site of the body to which such pressure is applied.

Direct external pressure

Occlusion of blood vessels can be caused by external pressure, which leads to tissue anoxia and the build-up of metabolites within both the cells and interstitial spaces. Relief of pressure causes a sudden increase in blood flow which can be as high as 30 times the resting tissue pressure (Bridel, 1993). The resultant increased blood flow causes the bright red flush characteristic of reactive hyperaemia. In health, vascular occlusion, though short-lived, regularly occurs especially in such areas of high pressure as the soles of the feet and the buttocks. However, where vascular occlusion occurs and remains unrelieved during illness which results in immobility or paralysis, tissues become permanently damaged. It is important to remember that both the intensity and duration of direct external pressure needs to be considered. Prolonged low, repeated short-lived low pressure and short-lived high pressure can all cause extensive damage. Direct external pressure, where prolonged, damages the lymphatic system, preventing the removal of excess interstitial fluid. The result is oedema, ineffective metabolite exchange, increasing tissue distortion and compression (Torrance, 1983).

Direct external pressure is often further compounded by the disruption of tissues and underlying structures from shear forces and friction.

Capillary closing pressures

This refers to the level of pressure required to damage the microcirculation. The figure quoted as the threshold for damage is 32mmHg (Landis, 1930). Therapies providing a level of pressure relief to maintain pressure below this threshold have been cited as preventing tissue breakdown. However, some caution needs to be exercised. The original research (Landis, 1930) was carried out using young, healthy, male volunteers and not the frail elderly or those with impaired autoregulatory processes. The vulnerability of individuals to capillary damage depends not only on the force required to close capillaries but also on their age and health. In addition, disruption of the tissues (by shear force and friction) which causes traumatic damage is also a factor.

Shear forces and friction

Previous studies suggest that shear forces can significantly add to the effect of externally-applied pressure in causing vascular occlusion, with the pressure level required to produce occlusion being reduced by 50% (Thomas et al., 1990). Interface pressure can be calculated by using the formula:

$$\text{Interface pressure} = \frac{\text{Patient weight}}{\text{Surface area supported}}$$

(Burman and O'Dea, 1994).

However, measuring interface pressure is difficult due to the currently available range of instruments used and the inaccuracies and inconsistencies of the measurements obtained (Garber and Krouskop, 1996).

Both shear forces and friction are responsible for damaging the arterioles and microcirculation. Shearing occurs when the skeleton and related tissues move over the skin, which remains static. An example of this happens when a seated patient slips down the chair. During shearing, the tissues move before the bony prominence but the support surface (chair or bed) stays still. This parallel pull rips the tissues and at the same time causes tissue distortion (Phillips, 1997). Friction, on the other hand, occurs when two surfaces rub together, an example being when a seated patient slips down the chair and is manually dragged back to an upright position. Poor manual handling and lifting techniques cause both friction and shear. In addition, excess sweating and incontinence increases moisture on the skin, which in turn increases the damage caused by friction and shear.

Risk assessment

The need to assess patients in a formal manner to determine whether or not there is a risk of tissue damage was first recognised in the late 1950s (Norton et al., 1962). Over a period of years, the concept of producing a risk-assessment scale, which could be widely used internationally, was developed; the Norton Pressure Ulcer Risk-Assessment Scale became freely available in 1979. Since that time many other risk assessment tools have become available (Flanagan, 1993a). The predictive abilities of these tools have been questioned and although useful, is not a substitute for sound clinical judgement (Flanagan, 1993a). A comparison of risk-assessment tools shows that impaired mobility is the only risk factor

---

Box 10.1 A comparison of pressure sore risk factors used in various risk assessment scales (Flanagan, 1993a)

Risk factor	Norton	Gosnall	Knoll	Waterlow	Braden
Mobility	✓	✓	✓	✓	✓
Activity	✓	✓	✓	✗	✓
Nutritional status	✗	✓	✓	✓	✓
Mental status	✓	✓	✓	✗	✓
Incontinence/moisture	✓	✓	✓	✓	✓
General physical condition	✓	✗	✓	✓	✗
Skin appearance	✗	✓	✗	✓	✗
Medication	✗	✓	✗	✓	✗
Friction/shear	✗	✗	✗	✗	✓
Weight	✗	✗	✗	✓	✗
Age	✗	✗	✗	✓	✗
Specific predisposing diseases	✗	✗	✓	✓	✗
Prolonged pressure	✗	✗	✗	✓	✗

common to five currently used tools (Norton, Gosnell, Knoll, Waterlow and Braden), with a range of other factors included (Box 10.1).

Although no tool can be accurate for all patient groups, the use of pressure ulcer risk-assessment tools can help nurses to identify vulnerable patients and also increase awareness of risk. A good risk-assessment tool will:

- Act as an *aide memoire* for carers
- Help provide data for audit purposes
- Provide evidence that prevention/treatment plans are based on objective criteria and a specific rationale
- Allow targeting of limited resources (Flanagan, 1993b).

The question of when and how often to use a risk-assessment tool has caused some controversy in the nursing world. Ideally, an assessment should be carried out as soon as possible following admission (within two hours) to hospital or on the first community visit (Phillips, 1997). This provides baseline information and also encourages early intervention. Thereafter, weekly assessments should suffice unless a significant change occurs in the patient's health status, including:

- Surgery
- Deterioration in general condition (mental or physical)
- Loss of appetite
- Presence of infection (wound, chest or urinary)
- Change in healthcare setting; transfer to community might mean lower nursing input
- Cardiac arrest or collapse from other causes (Phillips, 1997).

Classification and grading

The purpose of classifying and grading pressure ulcers by appearance and depth is to achieve a consensus or common language for describing and documenting the extent of tissue damage. This information is also useful for data collection and clinical audit. Several authors have devised classification systems (Torrance, 1983; DoH, 1993; Reid and Morison, 1994). However, in the UK, these have not been used on a nationwide basis. The EPUAP has adapted the NPUAP four-grade system (Box 10.2), and this is currently being widely disseminated throughout Europe.

EPUAP classification

In classifying tissue damage the number of grades and stages varies from 2 to 5. One important factor to consider, is whether the system includes non-blanching hyperaemia as a Stage 1 ulcer. Doing so raises the profile of the tissue damage in non-blanching hyperaemia (a difficult term and concept) to the status of a pressure ulcer, which is much easier to understand and may heighten the nurse's awareness of the risk of further tissue breakdown. This has also been shown to affect data collected for audit. In one study, including non-blanching hyperaemia as a Stage 1 ulcer gave a prevalence rate of 18.6%, while excluding it reduced the prevalence rate to 10.1% (O'Dea, 1993). The management of patients with pressure ulcers can be considered in four areas (Box 10.3).

Box 10.2 Pressure ulcer classification

Grade 1
Non-blanchable erythema of intact skin. Discolouration of the skin, warmth, oedema, induration or hardness may also be used as indicators, particularly on individuals with darker skin.

Grade 2
Partial thickness skin loss involving epidermis, dermis, or both. The ulcer is superficial and presents clinically as an abrasion or blister.

Grade 3
Full thickness skin loss involving damage to or necrosis of subcutaneous tissue that may extend down to, but not through underlying fascia.

Grade 4
Extensive destruction, tissue necrosis, or damage to muscle, bone, or supporting structures with or without full thickness skin loss.

Box 10.3 Management issues

Principle	Rationale
Relief of pressure (includes repositioning and manual handling)	Remove the source of the problem and prevent further damage
Control of intrinsic factors, e.g. diabetes, malnutrition	Rectifying factors which might impair healing will give the patient the best opportunity for rapid tissue repair
Identification of incontinence and promotion of continence	Wet, moist, contaminated skin is more at risk of further tissue breakdown
Appropriate local wound management	To provide the wound with an optimal environment for healing

Support surfaces

The aim of support surfaces (including both mattresses and cushions) is to protect the vulnerable patient from the adverse effects of external mechanical forces such as pressure, shear and friction. The clinical challenge for any nurse faced with a patient defined as being at risk of tissue damage is to ensure that the most appropriate support surfaces are used for that individual patient. In 1995, as many as 75 different beds and mattresses were commercially available (Dealey, 1995), though the strength of evidence supporting their use is weak. In a survey of 48 support systems, only two had been subjected to the rigours of a randomised controlled trial (Young, 1992). However, there is evidence suggesting that implementing guidelines in conjunction with equipment use reduces the incidence of pressure ulcers (Bale et al., 1996).

The choice of support surfaces is vast and includes overlay mattresses, replacement mattresses, beds and cushions. There is a range of technologies including air support systems, alternating air wave, dynamic air flotation, static air flotation and air-fluidised. It is helpful to match the level of patient risk to the type of support surface available.

Low level of risk

* Foam overlays/cushions
* Hollow core fibre overlays/cushions.

Medium level of risk

* Foam cushions
* Foam overlays
* Foam replacement mattresses.

Medium/high level of risk

* Air flotation overlays/cushions
* Alternating-pressure air overlays
* Gel mattresses/cushions
* Low-air loss overlay
* Static-air overlays/replacement mattresses/cushions.

High level of risk

* Air-fluidised beds
* Air wave mattresses
* Alternating-pressure air mattresses
* Dynamic air flotation mattresses
* Low-air loss mattresses/beds.

Many trusts and health boards in the UK have included flow charts in their guidelines in an attempt to help staff select the most appropriate equipment available within that area (Dealey, 1995). A more detailed breakdown of the ease of use, maintenance, ease of nursing procedure, patient acceptability and costs has been reported (Dealey, 1997), and includes overlays, mattresses, beds and cushions.

However, in addition to providing the most appropriate support surface for the patient's level of risk, regular repositioning of the patient must be ensured (Dealey, 1997). There is

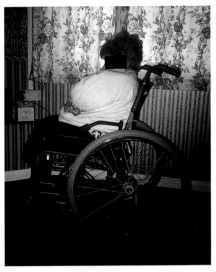

Figure 10.4 Patients with impaired mobility are at risk while sitting

currently no evidence demonstrating how frequently a patient needs to be repositioned or which methods to adopt. The following factors need to be considered in planning a repositioning strategy:

- The type of support surface the patient is being nursed on
- The patient's own ability to move (Figure 10.4)
- Disease aetiologies may prevent certain positioning, for example cardiac patients may encounter breathing difficulties or arthritic patients may experience pain when lying on their sides
- Staffing levels and the skill mix: poor manual handling can cause shearing and friction.

Mobility

Where possible, mobility of the patient should be a prime objective of care. Early referral to the physiotherapist and occupational therapist may promote this. The height of beds and chairs, proximity to toilet facilities and the use of devices such as frames and other walking aids can all help to increase the likelihood of mobility. As immobility has been identified as putting a patient at risk of tissue damage, careful consideration needs to be given to this aspect of patient care.

Control of intrinsic factors

Correcting or controlling disease aetiologies which have been cited as impairing wound healing or which predispose to tissue breakdown is essential. The nutritional health of the patient is also a key issue. Poor nutritional status, especially protein-energy malnutrition (PEM) is associated not only with hospitalisation but also with pressure ulcer development (McLaren, 1997). In patients with established pressure ulcers the problem of providing adequate nutrition is compounded by the loss of protein from the pressure ulcer in wound exudate. The larger the ulcer, the greater the problem.

Continence

Incontinence is associated with pressure ulcer development as it increases the vulnerability of damp skin to friction. For patients with an existing ulcer, there is an additional risk of wound contamination from urine and faeces. The advice of the continence advisor can be useful in both promoting continence and controlling incontinence.

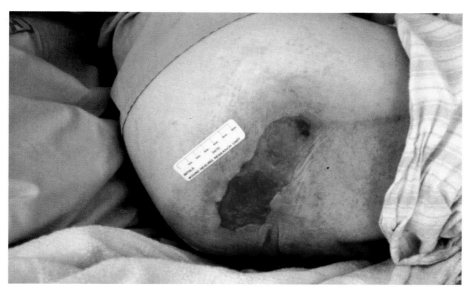

Figure 10.5 A healing Grade 4 pressure ulcer

Local wound management

The general principles of wound care should be followed (see Chapter 2). Specific problems encountered with managing pressure ulcers include poor wound shape and undermining of the skin edge (Figure 10.6), the presence of devitalised tissue and wound infection.

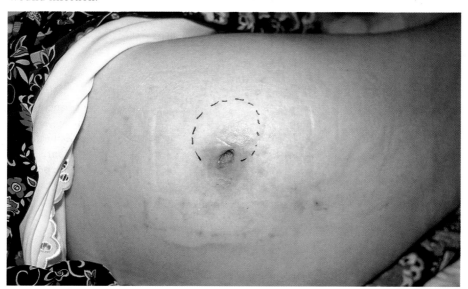

Figure 10.6 Extensive undermining mapped out on the patient's skin

The role of surgery

Due to the poor health and infirmity of many patients who develop pressure ulcers, surgery is not an appropriate option. The value of surgery should not be forgotten however, and for some patients referral to a general or plastic surgeon can be more appropriate than the use of conservative treatments. In countries outside the UK surgery is widely available and used, though only cited as being considered when the procedure will hasten the healing process, provide greater pain reduction or reduce costs (Kane, 1997). The range of surgical procedures used includes:
* Radical surgical debridement
* Primary closure
* Skin grafting
* Myocutaneous flap reconstruction
* Myofasciocutaneous flap reconstruction.

Prevention and management: a national and European issue

Over recent years, health service managers have become increasingly aware of the amount of resources used by patients who develop pressure ulcers and the rising costs associated with preventing them. In 1993, the Department of Health published *Pressure Ulcers: A key quality indicator*. This helped to raise the profile of the issues related to pressure ulcers and was used to provide information and guidance for NHS managers. A number of developments has brought managers and those caring directly for patients together:
* Clinical audit of pressure ulcers
* Development of policies by trusts
* Employment of tissue viability nurses and associated clinical nurse specialists
* Production of guidelines by trusts (Effective Health Care Bulletin, 1995).
* Production of guidelines by the Royal College of Nursing (2000).

The European Pressure Ulcer Advisory Board (EPUAP) was set up in 1996 to produce guidelines on the prevention and treatment of pressure ulcers; these have been disseminated throughout Europe. The EPUAP mission statement states that the panel exists to 'provide relief to persons suffering from or at risk of pressure ulcers, in particular through research and education of the public' (EPUAP, 1999). EPUAP members are active throughout Europe.

References

Bale, S., Finlay, I., Harding, K.G. (1992) Pressure ulcer prevention in a hospice. In: Cherry, G.W., Gottrup, F., Lawerence, J.C. et al. (eds) *Proceedings of the 5th European Conference on Advances in Wound Management*. London: Macmillan.

Bale, S., Jones, V. (1997) Wound care in the elderly individual with a pressure ulcer. In: *Wound Care Nursing: A patient-centred approach*. London: Balliere Tindall.

Bridel, J. (1993) The aetiology of pressure ulcers. *Journal of Wound Care* 2: 4; 230–238.

Bridel-Nixon, J. (1997) Pressure ulcers. In: Morison, M., Moffatt, C., Bridel-Nixon, J., Bale, S. (eds) *Nursing Management of Chronic Wounds*. London: Mosby.

Burman, P.M.S., O'Dea, K. (1994) Measuring pressure. *Journal of Wound Care* **3**: 283–286.

Callum, M.J., Harper, D.R., Dale, J.J. et al. (1987) Arterial disease in chronic leg ulceration: An underestimated hazard? Lothian and Forth Valley leg ulcer study. *British Medical Journal* **294**: 929–931.

Charcot, J.M. (1879) *Lectures on the diseases of the nervous system 'La Saltpetiere'*. Sigerson, G., Henry. C. (transl.). Lea: Philadelphia.

David, G., Chapman, R.G., Chapman, E.Z. et al. (1983) *An Investigation of the Current Methods Used in Nursing for the Care of Patients With Established Pressure Ulcers*. Harrow: Nursing Practice Unit.

Dealey, C. (1995) Mattresses and beds. *Journal of Wound Care* **4**: 9, 409–412.

Dealey, C. (1997) The politicisation of pressure ulcers In: *Managing Pressure Ulcer Prevention*. Guildford: Quay Books.

Department of Health (1993) *Pressure Ulcers: A key quality indicator*. London: Department of Health.

Effective Health Care Bulletin (1995) Prevention and Management of Pressure Ulcers 2:1. York: Churchill Livingstone and University of York.

European Pressure Ulcer Advisory Panel (1999) *Pressure Ulcer Treatment Guidelines*. Oxford: EPUAP.

Fabricius, G. (Hildanu Chirurgicus) (1593) *De gangaena et sphacelo tractus methodicus Leyden*.

Flanagan, M. (1993a) Pressure ulcer risk assessment scores. *Journal of Wound Care* **2**: 3, 162–166.

Flanagan, M. (1993b) Predicting pressure ulcer risk. *Journal of Wound Care* **2**: 4, 215–218.

Garber, S.L., Krouskop, T.A. (1996) The role of technology in pressure ulcer prevention. *Journal of Geriatric Dermatology* **4**: 5, 1891.

Hallet, A. (1996) Managing pressure ulcers in the community. *Journal of Wound Care* **5**: 3, 107.

Kane, D.P. (1997) Surgical Repair. In: Krasner, D., Kane, D. (eds) *Chronic Wound Care* (2nd ed.) Wayne, P.A.: health Management Publications Inc.

Landis, E.M. (1930) Micro-injection studies of capillary blood pressure in human skin. *Heart* **15**: 209–228.

Nightingale, F. (1861) *Notes on nursing*. New York: Appleton Century.

Norton, D., McLaren, R., Exton-Smith, A.N. (1962) *An Investigation of Geriatric Nursing Problems in Hospital*. Edinburgh: Churchill Livingstone.

O'Dea, K. (1993) Prevalence of pressure damage in hospitals in the UK. *Journal of Wound Care* **2**: 4, 221–225.

Office of Health Economics (1992) *Compendium of Health Care Statistics*. London: OHE.

Phillips, J. (1997) Causes of pressure ulcers In: *Pressure ulcers*. London: Churchill Livingstone.

Panel for the Prediction and Prevention of Pressure Ulcers. In: Adults (1992) *Pressure Ulcers in Adults: Prediction and prevention*. Clinical Practice Guideline No.3. Rockville Md: Agency for Health Care Policy and Research, US Department of Health and Human Services.

Reid, J., Morison, M. (1994) Towards a consensus classification of pressure sores. *Journal of Wound Care* **3**: 3, 151–160.

Scales, J.T. (1990) Pathogenesis of pressure ulcers. In: Bader, D.L. (ed.). *Pressure Ulcers*. London: Macmillan.

Schut, G.L. (1992) Diagnosis and treatment of decubitus In: *Advanced Wound Healing Resource*. Denmark: Coloplast.

Thomas, A., Krouskop, S.L., Noble, G. et al. (1990) Pressure management and the recumbent person. In: Bader, D.L. (ed.). *Pressure Ulcers*. London: Macmillan.

Thompson Rowling, J. (1961) Pathological changes in mummies. *Proceedings of the Royal Society of Medicine of London* **54**: 409.

Torrance, C. (1983) *Pressure Ulcers: Aetiology, treatment and prevention*. London: Croom Helm.

Young, J. (1992) The use of specialised beds and mattresses. *Journal of Tissue Viability* **2**: 3, 79–81.

Wound Care
in Practice

11. Case studies

Sue Bale and Keith Harding

This chapter outlines the case histories of six patients, with the aim of consolidating the information from previous chapters to illustrate how physiology, factors which affect healing, and wound characteristics can affect patient care. The wound management, dressings and problems of specific wound types are considered in a variety of physical and social environments. Each case study is presented in the same format:

* History
* Clinical challenges
* Treatment plan
* Outcome
* Discussion points.

Throughout the case studies, referral to previous chapters illustrates how the theory and knowledge gained from these chapters can be put into practice.

Case study 1: Drainage of a lactational breast abscess in a new mother

History

Mrs Cox recently gave birth to her third child. The labour was difficult and foetal distress led to the baby being delivered by emergency Caesarean section. Her previous two labours had been straightforward and resulted in vaginal delivery, and Mrs Cox had expected a similar experience with the third. She was therefore psychologically unprepared for the surgery, and distressed that it was needed. However, she was relieved that the baby was safely delivered, and made an uneventful postoperative recovery. She was able to breast-feed, and was discharged home to her husband and children on the sixth postoperative day.

Gradually, Mrs Cox's Caesarean incision site began to feel more comfortable, and over the following three weeks the baby breast-fed well and gained weight steadily. However, on the fourth week Mrs Cox began to feel unwell; she experienced flu-like symptoms and a sore right breast, from which the baby had difficulty feeding. Concerned about these symptoms, Mrs Cox went to see her GP. On examination the GP found a segment of the breast was red, inflamed and painful. Recognising that this could not be adequately managed conservatively he referred Mrs Cox for a surgeon's opinion. Following examination, the surgeon decided to admit Mrs Cox and her baby as an emergency.

By that evening Mrs Cox was feeling much worse; she had developed a spreading infection and was taken to theatre. She was given a general anaesthetic and a large breast abscess was drained, leaving a 2x3cm wound with a depth of 6cm. This was packed with Kaltostat as a haemostatic alginate. Although Mrs Cox was able to take her baby into hospital with her, she was advised to stop breast-feeding. Feeling tired, but much better, she was discharged to the care of the district nurse.

Clinical challenges

The wound Two major challenges faced the district nurse in managing this wound:
- Ongoing management of a deep and initially painful wound
- The need to keep the cavity open at the surface to allow healing by secondary intention
- Observation for signs of infection.

The patient The district nurse also had to take account of Mrs Cox's needs and circumstances:
- Mrs Cox needed emotional support; she was recovering from two surgical procedures (the Caesarean section and drainage of breast abscess), and had a new baby to care for and a young family
- There was the possibility of a generalised infection, for which Mrs Cox needed to be observed
- The breast wound was painful, and the district nurse needed to ensure pain relief was adequate.

The environment The nurse also needed to be aware that there were small children in the household and to pay special attention to the safe storage of equipment left in the home.

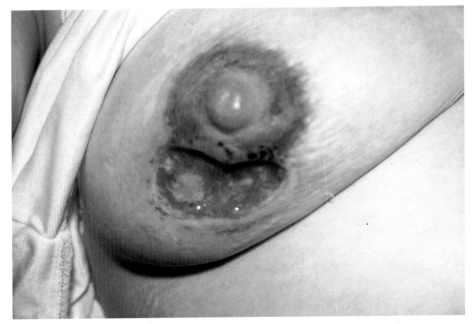

Figure 11.1 Mrs Cox's wound 3 weeks after surgery

Treatment plan

The district nurse formulated a treatment plan taking account of Mrs Cox's wound and individual circumstances:

- The wound was inspected daily for signs of pocketing and clinical signs of infection
- The wound dimensions were measured weekly
- The nurse liaised with the midwife/health visitor
- Visits were planned with Mrs Cox at a mutually convenient time.

On initial assessment the district nurse appreciated that Mrs Cox had experienced considerable trauma and needed a great deal of support in the coming weeks. She had undergone two operations with general anaesthetics, and now had a new baby and two other small children to care for and a home to run. Her husband had taken annual leave when the baby was born, but had now returned to work, though he managed much of the housework and took the older children to nursery and school on his way to work. Following assessment and redressing of the wound with alginate packing, the nurse arranged to call at the home at mutually convenient times.

Outcome

Over the next two weeks the wound made steady progress towards healing. The baby was now totally bottle-fed with formula milk and continued to gain weight steadily. Weekly wound measurements confirmed the wound was healing, and as it became smaller (Figure 11.1), Mrs Cox decided that she would like to undertake her own daily dressing changes, with the district nurse calling weekly to assess the wound. Five weeks following excision of the wound, epithelialisation was complete. Mrs Cox has now returned to normal activity and is enjoying her new baby.

Discussion points

The unexpected Caesarean section, followed by a breast abscess, resulted in Mrs Cox having two general anaesthetics in a short space of time. In addition, she had a new baby and two small children. Even with a supportive husband this was an extremely stressful time for her. An often overlooked aspect of care is the role of the patient's spouse or relative undertaking dressing changes and in this case it was entirely appropriate to encourage this when the wound was healing well. The district nurse took all this into account when planning Mrs Cox's care, and was able to offer a service suited to her circumstances.

Case study 2: Care of a patient with a venous leg ulcer in the community

Mrs Price, aged 55 years, was active and recently retired from her part-time job as a shop assistant. After the birth of her two children 30 years ago she had developed varicose veins

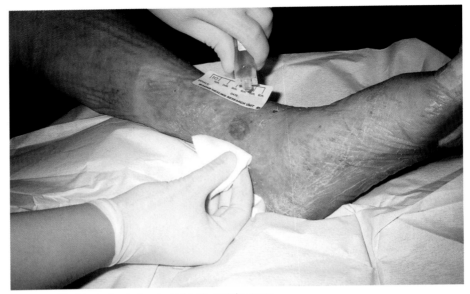

Figure 11.2 Mrs Price's ulcer being cleaned by the practice nurse

on both legs. These had caused no problems but Mrs Price had noticed an increasingly prominent staining around her ankles.

Whilst cleaning her home she injured her right leg. The bleeding quickly subsided, but rather than healing over the next few days, she noticed that the wound was increasing in size. Somewhat alarmed, Mrs Price made an appointment to see her GP. On presentation at the surgery she had a healthy 6x4cm wound on her left medial malleolus.

Clinical challenges

Lower limb assessment This can be undertaken at the surgery with the practice nurse and GP.

GP assessment History-taking, physical examination (all pulses present from femoral down to pedal).

Nursing assessment This involved a number of procedures:
- Urinalysis, to exclude diabetes; this was negative
- Doppler assessment for APBI; this was 1.1, indicating venous disease
- Tracing and measuring the ulcer; this was 6x4cm
- Measurement of ankle and mid-calf circumference to help select an appropriately-sized bandage
- Ascertain Mrs Price's views on and compliance with compression bandaging.

With these investigations complete the GP and nurse discussed the diagnosis and possible treatment options. As the primary diagnosis was venous ulceration, the main aim of treatment was to reduce oedema in the affected leg by applying compression therapy.

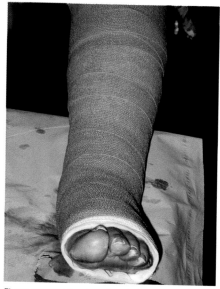

Figure 11.3 The four-layer bandaging system in place

Following consultation with Mrs Price, the first line of treatment was four-layer compression bandages and non-adherent textile dressings. Bandages and dressings were subsequently prescribed by the GP, while the practice nurse assumed responsibility for Mrs Price's ongoing care at the surgery.

Treatment plan

The treatment plan involved a range of interventions:

- Skin care with 50% liquid and 50% soft white paraffin
- Primary dressing with non-adherent textile dressing
- Compression therapy with four-layer bandages
- Encouragement to continue to walk and exercise regularly
- Dressing changes to be performed at the surgery, as Mrs Price was happy to walk from her home nearby
- Ongoing patient education on the disease process and care that the leg will need following healing.

At each weekly assessment the ulcer was traced, the wound assessed, the leg and foot washed and moisturising cream applied to the lower leg. As the weeks went by the nurse took the opportunity to explain the nature of venous disease and long-term care of the limb following healing. Mrs Price was also taught ankle and calf muscle pump exercises, which assist venous return. As the ulcer healed, dressing change frequency was reduced to weekly.

Outcome

After nine weeks of treatment the ulcer was completely re-epithelialised. The GP prescribed Class 2 compression stockings as long-term treatment for Mrs Price. The local pharmacist measured Mrs Price's foot and leg, supplied and fitted her stocking.

Discussion points

Mrs Price presented with a typical history of venous disease and ulceration, and examination and investigation confirmed the diagnosis of venous ulceration. With the doctor and nurse working as a team, in conjunction with the patient, they discussed methods of treatment and selected an appropriate compression bandaging system. The issues of patient mobility and compliance were also addressed and led to a successful outcome. Although this was the first episode of ulceration for Mrs Price, she may experience recurrence on several occasions due to the nature of the disease. Knowing this, the nurse took the time to build up a relationship with Mrs Price and used the opportunity to provide ongoing health education.

Case study 3: Managing a patient with vascular disease and ulceration

History

Mr Smith, a widower aged 63, had smoked from the age of 11, and throughout his youth and middle age had led an active life with no major illnesses. However, at the age of 61 he noticed that he had to stop on his way to the shops due to a painful cramp in his left calf. Over the following two years this progressively worsened and Mr Smith was able to walk no more than 100 metres without stopping. On presentation to his GP, a provisional diagnosis of intermittent claudication was made, and he was referred to a vascular surgeon. Examination and further investigation with a duplex scan at the hospital revealed widespread arterial disease with poor distal blood vessels. As the vascular disease was widespread and thought to be related to long-term cigarette smoking, reconstructive surgery or angioplasty was not indicated. Mr Smith was advised to stop smoking immediately and was given oral analgesics to ease his pain.

Mr Smith's extended family was able to give support by undertaking his housework, and regularly took him out by car. During an outing to the coast Mr Smith stumbled and fell against a stone wall. His daughter treated the small resultant laceration with antiseptic cream and noticed a small area of bruising in the surrounding area. During the following 48 hours the area became red and swollen and the wound opened up and began oozing a malodorous discharge. Alarmed at this sudden deterioration, Mr Smith telephoned his GP, who visited him at home. Realising the problems of treating Mr Smith with oral antibiotics due to the impaired blood supply to the limb, the GP admitted him to the local hospital. On admission, Mr Smith was exhibiting both systemic and local signs of infection with a tachycardia, pyrexia and an erythematous, swollen limb with a malodorous discharge.

Clinical challenges

The ward nurse needed to take account of a number of factors in caring for the wound:
- The length, breadth and depth of the wound was measured
- The extent of the erythema was drawn with an ink marker on the leg; the erythema was observed four-hourly and retraced if it had extended
- A bacteriological swab was taken for culture and sensitivity
- Blood cultures were taken for culture and sensitivity
- Blood tests were taken for white cell count, renal and liver function
- An alginate dressing was covered with absorbent pads and these were held in place with a light retention bandage.

Mr Smith also required a number of other interventions:

- A broad-spectrum, intravenous antibiotic was commenced until bacteriological results were available
- Four-hourly temperature, pulse and respiration were recorded
- Four-hourly limb assessment was undertaken to observe for circulatory changes to the foot
- Strong analgesia was provided as required and Mr Smith was reassessed regularly for pain.

Treatment plan

Again the treatment plan took account of the condition of Mr Smith's wound and his individual circumstances:

- A non-adherent textile dressing was covered with soft padding, and held in place with a light cotton retention bandage (Chapter 5)
- Initally the wound was observed twice daily and this continued until the wound began to improve
- Dressing changes were planned to coincide with maximum analgesic effect.

Over the following 24 hours Mr Smith's condition improved with the systemic and local signs of infection settling. Blood cultures were negative and the wound swab showed a mixed growth of aerobic organisms including *Staphylococcus aureus* and Group G Streptococcus. The erythema surrounding the wound slowly resolved and the wound became less prolific, without odour. Dressings, which initially needed changing twice daily, were left in place for 48 hours. Intravenous antibiotics were replaced by oral drugs until the end of the course.

Mr Smith was discharged back to the care of his GP and district nurse. He needed:

- Oral antibiotics to complete course
- Dressing changes and limb assessments every second day
- Wound assessment and evaluation with continuing care.

Outcome

Four months later the ulcer was unhealed, though smaller and free from infection. Over this period the district nurse reinforced advice given by the GP and hospital for Mr Smith to stop smoking (Chapter 2) and to take an active interest in the condition and health of his feet and legs. Mr Smith's son took him to the chiropodist every six weeks and paid for this service as well as taking him in the car. The extended family took an active interest in the disease and was eager to be educated on the causes and problems of smoking-related diseases. Mr Smith's son gave up smoking to help his father and was very supportive during the process.

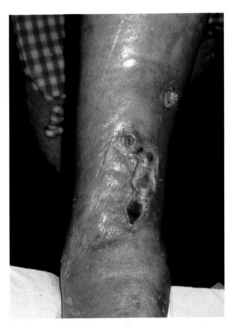

Figure 11.4 Mr Smith's unhealed ulcer, four months following injury

Discussion points

With the gradual onset of ischaemic disease Mr Smith had difficulty relating smoking to the disease process. However, once he became acutely ill he appreciated the severity of the disease, as did his extended family. The support from the district nurse with ongoing health education had a positive and beneficial effect in this situation.

With ischaemic disease, sudden deterioration of an infected injury is not uncommon. It was important that the GP did not attempt to treat Mr Smith with oral antibiotics and manage him in the community. In-patient treatment was appropriate, with regular inspection of the limb to observe for further deterioration which, left untreated, could have led to septicaemia or amputation, and could even have been fatal.

Wound assessment and management were carried out and reviewed regularly. Dressings were changed as appropriate, more frequently during the acute illness when exudate was copious and malodorous; as the wound improved dressings were changed less frequently.

Case study 4: Management of a patient with deep pressure ulcers

History

Mrs Simons, aged 74 years, lived at home with her husband. Previously well, over a period of two weeks she had become increasingly short of breath and spent much of her day sitting in a chair, or remaining in bed. Worried about his wife, Mr Simons contacted the GP for a home visit. Following examination the GP made a preliminary diagnosis of severe congestive cardiac failure, and decided to admit Mrs Simons to hospital for further investigation and treatment.

Whilst admitting Mrs Simons the ward nurse noticed two large Stage 3 sacral pressure ulcers measuring 8x5 cms and covered with sloughy material. In addition to loss of mobility Mrs Simons reported having lost her appetite and not drinking her usual amounts of fluids. At this time her Waterlow score was calculated to be very high at 23.

Clinical challenges

The wound

- Wound size and site were documented in the nursing notes as being present at the time of admission. The measurements formed the baseline for future assessments
- On admission, necrotic tissue was present on the wound bed; again, this was documented and the need for wound debridement noted.

The patient

Mrs Simons also required a number of other interventions:

- With a Waterlow risk score of 23, Mrs Simons was rated as being at very high risk of further tissue damage; an appropriate pressure-relieving mattress and chair cushion were needed, and both were provided according to the trust's policy
- Whilst waiting for baseline biochemical investigations to be processed, the dietitian was asked to carry out a full nutritional assessment and to formulate a dietary plan
- Although the wound was not painful on admission, this required monitoring
- Assessment of mobility was not appropriate at the time of admission, the physiotherapist was made aware of Mrs Simon's future needs
- Medical management included baseline haematology and biochemistry, a plain X-ray of sacrum, diuretics, digoxin and oxygen therapy.

Treatment plan

- Ongoing pressure support and turning/repositioning
- Provision of adequate fluids and nutrition
- Regular reassessment of risk score (Waterlow).

The treatment plan focused on improving the wound's condition to optimise healing, and avoiding infection:

- Daily application of a hydrogel to encourage autolytic debridement of the devitalised, necrotic tissue from the wound bed
- Daily inspection for the early detection of wound infection or more seriously spreading infection in the surrounding tissues; this might herald the advent of systemic infection, a potentially fatal condition
- Sharp debridement of loosening necrotic tissue to help speed up the debridement process.

On admission Mrs Simons' serum albumin was 25gm/L; 21 days later this had risen to 32 and, at 40 days was 36. At this time Mrs Simons felt much better, and was eating and drinking normally. Her Waterlow score had fallen to 11 and she was nursed on a foam overlay mattress. The sacral sore debrided completely after 13 days and was healing rapidly (Figure 11.5). Exudate production was diminishing and the hydrogel was replaced with a hydrocolloid sheet. Mrs Simons found the hydrocolloid dressing comfortable and appreciated the convenience of being able to shower without requiring a dressing change.

Outcome

Mrs Simons' mobility gradually returned to normal and she was well enough to be discharged home from hospital three weeks after admission. The district nurse was called to monitor her progress and to assess and manage the wound. Dressing changes were needed only every five days, and wound assessment was undertaken at that time. Five weeks after being discharged home Mrs Simons' pressure sore was completely healed.

Discussion points

During the course of her acute illness, Mrs Simons' physical condition rapidly deteriorated. Because of the nature of her illness she sat upright in her chair, without either she or her husband realising that a large area of tissue damage had developed. A combination of unrelieved pressure and illness resulted in a potentially hazardous situation for Mrs Simons. Had urgent medical and nursing treatment not been given she may well have developed septicaemia and died from complications of the pressure ulcer.

A thorough physical medical and nursing assessment preceded active treatment. In the days which followed, Mrs Simons gradually recovered and her treatment was modified accordingly. Dressing change frequency and the amount of pressure relief was reduced over this period. It was important to Mrs Simons that she quickly recovered her independence and could be discharged home to her husband. Frequent assessment of the patient and her risk of further tissue damage was an essential part of her nursing care. As the risk of this diminished Mrs Simons' care was tailored to meet her own, individual

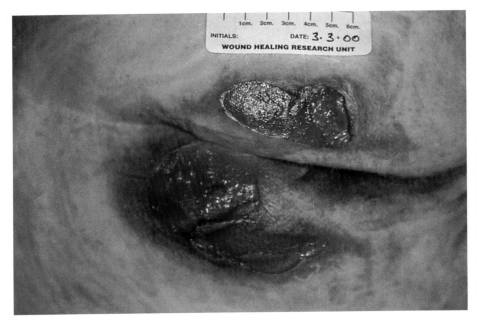

Figure 11.5 Mrs Simon's wound

needs. The wound initially required debridement; once this was achieved, it was acceptable to use a hydrocolloid dressing throughout the whole of Mrs Simons' healing phase. The sacral area is difficult to dress and this self-adhesive type of dressing provided comfort and convenience in this situation.

Case study 5: Caring for a patient following a traumatic injury

History

Mr Jones, a 32-year-old car mechanic, had accidentally fired a high-pressure oil gun at his abdomen whilst at work. His colleagues took him immediately to the A&E department of the local hospital. Mr Jones' dirty clothes were soaked with oil and stuck to his abdomen, and he was in considerable pain. He was admitted immediately and his clothes were cut away from the injured area before he was taken to theatre. The full extent of his injuries were assessed and radical wound debridement of the area undertaken under general anaesthetic. The large wound was packed with a haemostatic alginate rope.

A tetanus injection was administered on the ward as the original injury occurred in a dirty environment, and he had not received tetanus phrophylaxis within the previous 10 years. Mr Jones stayed in hospital for 48 hours. The first alginate pack was changed 24 hours after surgery, as it was saturated with exudate and some blood. The pack was loosened whilst Mr Jones lay in a warm, saline bath, and fell out of the wound spontaneously. Seeing the wound for the first time, Mr Jones' initial reaction was of shock at the extent of the tissue damage to his abdomen; the wound measured 15x17cm and was 5cm deep. Having a wife and small children to support, Mr Jones was anxious to be discharged from hospital as quickly as possible, so that he could return to work.

Clinical challenges

The wound was to be managed by the district nurse following Mr Jones' discharge from hospital. Wound management involved managing exudate, monitoring progress, minimising the risk of infection, and using appropriate dressings:

- The large volume of exudate was contained by daily packing with alginate rope, covered with a large absorbent pad and held in place with small amounts of surgical tape
- Progress towards healing was monitored by measuring the maximum length, breadth and depth on a weekly basis
- The wound was monitored at each dressing change for the clinical signs of infection
- As the wound healed and exudate levels reduced frequency of dressing change was modified.

Mr Jones also needed a care plan that took account of his circumstances:

- Mr Jones had never been in hospital before, and together with the extent of his surgery, this made him understandably anxious and in need of support and encouragement
- Pain was initially controlled using an intravenous patient-controlled system to administer morphine; after 24 hours this was discontinued and replaced with oral analgesia, the effectiveness of which was monitored by the district nurse
- Mr Jones needed to return to work as quickly as possible in order to support his family.

Environmental factors were also taken into consideration: whilst Mr Jones was at home, wound contamination was not considered to be an issue. However, on his return to work, in a dirty, dusty environment there was the potential for wound contamination.

Treatment plan

Week 1 The wound was dressed with alginate packing with absorbent padding, held in place with surgical tape. Mr Jones was discharged from hospital on the second day postoperatively. He was adjusting to the presence of the wound; he was comfortable with the dressing in place and able to walk without undue discomfort. The district nurse visited the following morning and undertook a full assessment; Mr Jones' priority was to return to work as quickly as possible. In the following days he gradually regained normal mobility, and on the seventh day planning began in earnest for him to return to work.

Week 2 The district nurse felt the most appropriate dressing to enable self-care and return to work was a foam cavity wound dressing. She arranged to call weekly at the home to make a new dressing and assess the progress of the wound towards healing.

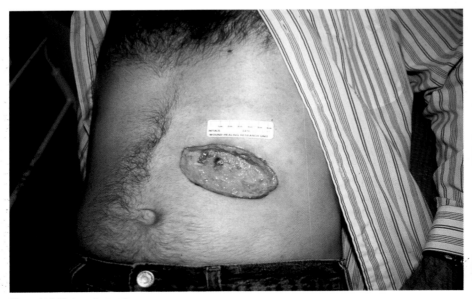

Figure 11.6 Mr Jones' wound

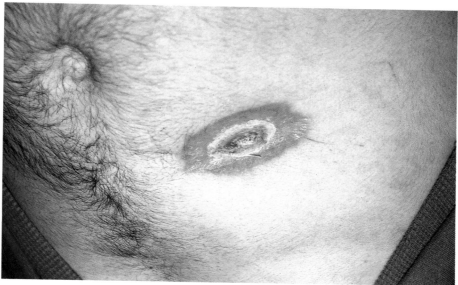

Figure 7.1 The wound after 6 weeks

The nature of Mr Jones' work meant that contamination of the granulating wound was a potential problem. To reduce this risk a semipermeable film dressing was used to secure the foam dressing in place, whilst acting as a barrier to dust and dirt.

Outcome

Over the following four weeks Mr Jones undertook the day-to-day care of his wound. The district nurse visited weekly to assess the wound. During the last week of healing, whilst the wound completed epithelialisation, the semipermeable film was used as the primary contact material.

Discussion points

Despite suffering significant tissue loss, Mr Jones made a rapid recovery. The use of a haemostatic alginate was useful in the immediate postoperative stage, but when it was clear that Mr Jones wanted an early discharge home and to care for his own wound, an alternative needed to be found. The involvement of the district nurse was necessary in the early days as Mr Jones had a large defect in his abdominal wall, which needed close monitoring. In addition he may have felt insecure and anxious on discharge from hospital at having to take sole responsibility for his wound care.

The advice and support of the district nurse gave Mr Jones confidence. Some problems in returning to work were anticipated, the dirty working environment being the main difficulty. The combined use of a patient-manageable dressing and a film dressing to prevent wound contamination met Mr Jones' needs in this situation.

Case study 6: Management of a foot wound in a patient with diabetes

History

Mr Williams, a 51-year-old self-employed carpenter, had a 30-year history of diabetes mellitus. Although he was careful to maintain his diabetic control with insulin, he had previously been resistant to participating in ongoing monitoring for diabetes-related complications (in particular eye disease and foot complications).

On returning home one evening, Mr Williams took off his work boots to find one saturated with blood. On closer inspection he found a nail in the sole of his boot and a puncture wound on the sole of his foot; due to peripheral neuropathy, he had not appreciated the injury at the time. Unaware of the importance of seeking early treatment for a dirty, traumatic injury, Mr Williams merely bathed his foot and applied an adhesive plaster; 24 hours later he felt systemically unwell, was feverish, and noticed that his foot was swollen and red. He immediately went to his GP, who admitted him to hospital for urgent investigation and treatment.

At the hospital, plain X-rays of the foot and blood tests for baseline biochemical and haematological markers were taken, and broad spectrum intravenous antibiotics were commenced. The X-rays showed a large, fluid-filled cavity in the sole of the foot, and the blood test results showed evidence of systemic infection. Radical debridement was undertaken in theatre under a general anaesthetic, resulting in a large cavity wound measuring 8x5cm and 2cm deep. This was packed in theatre with a haemostatic alginate rope, covered with soft, absorbent padding and held in place with a cotton retention bandage.

Clinical challenges

The wound A number of nursing challenges were presented:
- In the immediate postoperative period bleeding needed to be monitored
- The health of the wound bed also required regular monitoring at dressing changes; the size had to be measured weekly throughout the healing process, and build-up of slough had to be noted and debrided
- Infection is the major potential complication for the diabetic foot patient; in addition to early detection of the clinical signs of infection in the wound bed, the foot and lower leg need also needed to be carefully observed for signs of spreading infection, as the neuropathy associated with diabetes can mask the pain normally felt in the sensate foot
- This was a large cavity wound, producing a considerable quantity of exudate
- Throughout the healing phase, pressure-relieving/offloading footwear was needed to reduce local pressure; Mr Williams will also require specialised footwear following complete healing
- Callus build-up would continue at the wound edge throughout healing, and would require active debridement at least every two weeks.

A number of other considerations were taken into account:

- Close monitoring of Mr Williams' blood sugars and the appropriate use of insulin were required in the immediate postoperative period; as he recovered, the infection settled and a normal eating pattern returned; his usual insulin/diet regimen could then be resumed
- Due to the nature and extent of the infection in the leg, close observation for systemic infection was required
- Although there was some degree of neuropathy in Mr Williams' foot, pain needed to be monitored and analgesia given as needed
- Mr Williams was alarmed at the speed at which his foot deteriorated following what he perceived to be a minor and trivial injury; he needed support to help him come to terms with this and to reduce feelings of guilt
- Mr Williams was extremely receptive to education at this time and wished to prevent such an event from happening again; the diabetic specialist nurse was able to support the ward nurse in providing such education.

The environment This also required consideration. Whilst in hospital Mr Williams was protected from many hazards to his wound, including walking, by being encouraged to bed rest, while close monitoring of his diabetes, wound and leg would identify complications early. However, Mr Williams was self-employed and anxious to return to work as soon as possible after discharge. He was fortunate in that a multidisciplinary foot clinic was held at his local hospital, and once discharged he could have regular appointments. Temporary pressure-relieving footwear was provided, to a safety standard that allowed him to return to work on a building site whilst a more appropriate long-term footwear solution was ordered. The deleterious effects of such an early return to work were likely to impact on the rate of

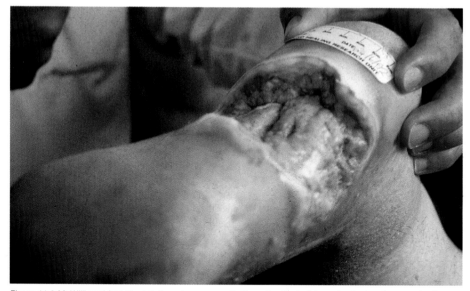

Figure 11.8 Mr Williams' foot at week 3 post-surgery; note the extensive build-up of callus on the wound edge

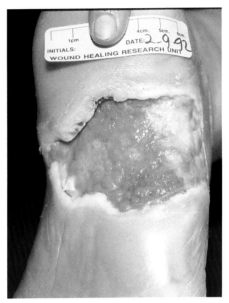

Figure 11.9 As the ulcer healed, callus continued to build up

Figure 11.10 The healed foot

healing, therefore a compromise was made with the foot clinic. Mr Williams returned to work but agreed to return weekly to clinic for wound assessment, debridement, callus removal and ongoing monitoring of his diabetes.

Treatment plan

Immediately following surgery, haemostatic alginate rope was used to both encourage haemostasis and absorb exudate. This was covered with a soft absorbent pad and held in place with a cotton retention bandage.

While Mr Williams was in hospital, use of alginate rope was continued to fill the cavity and absorb exudate. Whilst the wound remained a cavity this dressing was suitable.

Once Mr Williams was discharged home with a flat wound, absorbent foam dressings were used. The exudate reduced, and Mr Williams returned to work. This led to the additional factor of potential contamination needing to be considered. The building site was dirty and dusty and there was a need for both occlusion and antimicrobial dressings. An iodine-impregnated textile dressing was used as a prophylactic measure in conjunction with absorbent padding. This was changed daily for inspection of the foot.

Outcome

Mr Williams was discharged from hospital four weeks after surgery. He performed his dressing changes with the help of his wife, who closely inspected the foot for signs of infection. Over the next four months, the wound made slow progress to healing. Visits to the foot clinic were reduced in frequency over this time. In patients with diabetes healing is inevitably slow, but as the foot clinic could arrange convenient appointments Mr Williams was able to return to work. Once complete healing was achieved he continued to attend the foot clinic for monitoring.

Discussion points

The sudden and unexpected onset of his illness surprised and distressed Mr Williams. Several aspects of care needed to be addressed concurrently, namely, control of diabetes, monitoring of infection, foot care and wound care. Management of hospital discharge was very much patient-led, with Mr Williams returning to work early. The foot clinic staff, whilst recognising that healing was likely to be prolonged, worked with Mr Williams to develop a care package which allowed this.

12. The nurse specialist in wound management

Sue Bale

Providing nursing care in today's healthcare setting may produce many problems, mainly in relation to financial constraints and new management structures. However, there are many opportunities for nurses to develop new skills, enabling them to deliver flexible and effective wound care, as well as a wide range of other nursing activities. By developing an understanding of, and reacting positively to, change, nurses can continue to develop their profession. One of the pathways to success is through developing existing pre- and post-registration education.

Wound management is essentially a multidisciplinary effort, with individual members of the healthcare team working in partnership with patients. However, the majority of patients with wounds interact most with the nurse, who delivers much of their wound intervention. Nurses are, therefore, ideally placed to lead the team for many patients with wounds. In line with government policy outlined in *The NHS Plan* (DoH, 2000), the role of the nurse is becoming increasingly important in the NHS. Professional bodies have also supported and defined specialist and advanced nursing practice (UKCC, 1995).

This chapter addresses the role of the clinical nurse specialist (CNS), multiprofessional teams, education, methods of evaluating care and the use of guidelines.

The role of the clinical nurse specialist

For nurses working in wound care, as well as other areas of nursing, the emergence of a range of CNS roles has been a significant development (Hutton, 1997). These nurses have been shown to be of benefit in many areas of nursing, with improved quality of patient care being achieved when they contribute to nursing care (Wright, 1991).

It is generally recognised that CNSs perform a variety of roles which were first described by Storr (1988), followed by Wright (1991). Storr (1988) identified five commonly accepted sub-roles of the CNS:

- Practitioner: the CNS acts as a role model for general nurses, and is able to assess patients comprehensively and develop nursing care plans based on advanced clinical knowledge and expertise
- Educator: the CNS can educate patients, families, nursing staff, and other healthcare team members
- Consultant: consultation can be both formal and informal, and is most effective when the CNS is readily available or highly visible to the nursing staff
- Researcher: initiating and carrying out research is part of the specialist role; the CNS is ideally placed to evaluate research findings for implementation in practice
- Change agent: the CNS is expected to act as a catalyst for change within the organisation to improve patient care, promote communication and improve nursing practice.

Wright (1991) identified a number of aims for the specialist/advanced practitioner:

- The continuing development of the profession in the interests of patients, clients and the health service
- Adjusting the boundaries for the development of future practice
- Pioneering and developing new roles that are responsive to changing needs
- Advancing clinical practice, research and education to enrich nursing practice as a whole
- Contributing to health policy and the management and determination of health needs.

The number of CNSs in wound care in the UK is increasing, as both hospital and community trusts realise the benefits of such nurses (Flanagan, 1992). This growth has been relatively rapid: a postal survey (Flanagan, 1997) found that the first appointment of a tissue viability nurse was in 1983, but by 1997, 110 had been appointed. Some 90% of the respondents were in newly created posts, and Flanagan highlighted some of the difficulties of having so many new practitioners in the field, including the lack of available role models.

Castledine (1992) described specialist nurses as recognisable, accountable experts who can lead, or be consulted, because of their in-depth knowledge and skill. The wound care specialist has been described as having a unique role to play as an educator, researcher, practitioner and consultant (Hollingworth, 1993).

The specialist-generalist debate

The development of the CNS within wound care has not been without its problems. These include:

- Some general nurses perceive them to be protective of their special skills and knowledge to the extent that they are unwilling to share them with others (Bale, 1995)
- Flanagan (1997) found that 76% of CNSs who responded to her postal survey reported that they often felt stressed, with 44% feeling professionally isolated from their peers; Flanagan recommended that a professional network be set up for peer support (for example tissue viability nurses societies/groups).

Generalists also argue that the introduction of a increasing range of specialists will fragment nursing care, while specialists point to evidence of the benefits that they impart in their extended role. The effectiveness of CNSs in terms of faster patient recovery, shorter hospital stays, improved staff morale and better patient outcomes has been reported (Elder and Bullock, 1990). Regardless of personal views, generalist and specialist are urged to work effectively together to provide holistic care for their patients (Hollingworth, 1993).

Flanagan (1992) outlined a draft proposal for the CNS role in wound care, to reduce the ambiguity so often encountered in the specialty (Box 12.1).

Box 12.1 A CNS for wound care (Flanagan, 1992)

General aim of post

To develop a high standard of nursing practice based on the principles of research-based individualised nursing care.

Main responsibilities

- To act as a resource for staff in wound management practice and research, while undertaking an advisory role for senior management
- To act as a role model for clinical nurses
- To initiate and participate in clinical research and evaluation as appropriate
- To promote research-based practice with the aim of improving care
- To evaluate current research and practice to assess the effectiveness of available preventive care treatment options
- To initiate appropriate changes in patient care in response to current developments in wound management, and to liaise with nurses/managers to ensure that these are achieved
- To support staff and facilitate understanding of current developments in wound management, and to bring these to the attention of senior management as appropriate
- To identify existing wound management resources and services
- To identify educational needs and to plan, implement and evaluate education programmes involving all relevant members of the team, liaising with the continuing education department as appropriate
- To develop training contracts with provider units and other agencies related to wound management
- To raise awareness of ethical/legal issues related to wound management and reflect this in clinical practice
- To liaise with other specialists at local level and develop and maintain links with relevant agencies and organisations at national and international level
- To assist in the co-ordination of quality assurance programmes and to facilitate the formulation, implementation and auditing of clinical standards relating to wound management
- To review, formulate and implement policies and guidelines
- To assess and evaluate wound care products and equipment in order to promote cost-effective and high-quality services
- To advise budget holders on the most cost-effective preventive care and treatment options available
- To co-ordinate the allocation of relevant resources with the appropriate managers and in accordance with agreed policy
- To negotiate with suppliers for the provision of appropriate equipment/dressings for the effective management of wounds

The CNS is able to co-ordinate and facilitate care for individual patients, and can use a system of formal and informal contacts to work around bureaucratic obstacles for the benefit of the patient (Humpris, 1994). Nurse specialists in wound care can interact with other members of the healthcare team involved in the care of a particular patient, and often have highly developed interpersonal skills which help them to gain the support of other professions.

In the management of wounds and wound problems the CNS is ideally placed to assess the patient's needs and develop an individualised treatment plan. Often it is the drive and enthusiasm of the CNS which helps to make the treatment plan happen. This may be achieved in a number of ways (Bale, 1995):

- By using the skills of the most appropriate professional to ensure that an accurate diagnosis is obtained
- By ensuring that treatment is planned in partnership with those delivering care, making the plan as practical as possible; this will take into account the physical environment in which the patient is being cared for, and the choice and availability of treatment and dressing materials
- By monitoring and auditing the effectiveness of care
- By acting as a facilitator and liaising with other healthcare professionals as and when appropriate, facilitating an optimal standard of care for individual patients
- By following patients' progress to healing, to ensure that appropriate continuing treatment and ongoing care is delivered even after discharge from hospital to the care of community nurses.

Multiprofessional teams

Wound care is an ideal specialty in which to encourage and promote the multiprofessional team approach to patient care. Patients with wounds and wound problems are found in all areas of medicine and nursing, from neonatal intensive care units through to elderly care environments both in hospital and in the community (Bale and Jones, 1997). Although nurses generally have most direct contact with patients with wounds, the role of other professionals must be recognised and their services called upon as and when appropriate. There are three wound aetiologies where the multiprofessional team approach is well developed and its effectiveness demonstrated: the diabetic foot care team; leg ulcer services; and tissue viability services (Box 12.2).

The multiprofessional team approach has also been reported as effective in other, less well-established areas of wound care, including community-based teams (O'Flynn, 1997) and a bone infection unit (Sutherland, 1997).

The diabetic foot team

The effectiveness of a well-organised multidisciplinary foot-care team was first reported in 1986 (Edmonds et al., 1986). Other centres internationally have modified the approach described in this seminal paper as a cost-effective system for delivering care to patients

---

Box 12.2 Multiprofessional teams working in wound care, and their members

Diabetic foot care
- Diabetologist
- Orthopaedic surgeon
- General practitioner
- The patient
- Orthotist
- Community/practice nurses
- Diabetes nurse specialist
- Hospital nurses
- Chiropodist/podiatrist
- Vascular surgeon

Leg ulcer services
- General practitioner
- Vascular nurse specialist
- Community/practice nurses
- The patient
- Dermatologist

- Hospital nurses
- Vascular surgeon
- Nurse specialists

Tissue viability teams
- Tissue viability nurse
- Physician
- Physiotherapist
- The patient
- Ward nurses
- Dietitian/nutritionalist
- Occupational therapist
- Continence nurse
- Plastic surgeon
- General practitioner
- Community/practice nurses
- Geriatrician
- Medical rehabilitationist

These teams share certain goals and structures:
- Clear roles for individual team members
- Identification of the team leader
- Clear pathways for patient referrals
- Mutually agreed standards (which can be audited)
- Production and use of guidelines/protocols

---

with this costly clinical problem (Connor, 1994; Middleton et al., 1995; Knowles et al., 1996). An expansion of this approach, with a wider range of professional team members and case conferences following each clinic (to design individual, integrated care plans) has been reported (Sibbald et al., 1996).

Leg ulcer services

Based on another seminal piece of research, the Riverside Community Leg Ulcer Project (Blair et al., 1988), the first community-based, comprehensive leg ulcer service was set up. This service was new and innovative in that a comprehensive service was developed within a community network which liaised closely with a vascular surgical service. Since then, other leg ulcer services, mostly community-based and nurse-led (but with an easy pathway into hospital services) have been set up (Lambourne, 1996).

Tissue viability services

It has been recommended that for the effective treatment of patients at risk of or with pressure ulcers, a multiprofessional approach should be used (Browning, 1997). Buchbinder et al. (1997) recognised not only that effective wound care programmes provide an optimal environment for healing, but also that a team of dedicated individuals with specialist training is essential. Although such authors recommend the provision of a purpose-built centre for wound care, this is not essential. Collaboration and co-operation between the participating professional groups, both in hospital and in the community, are more important factors in providing effective services.

The success of the first wound clinic in the UK, set up in 1972, reported an increase in numbers and types of referral to a multiprofessional team (Harding and Bale, 1997). The development of this unit, staffed by physicians, surgeons, specialist nurses, educationalists and researchers in a university hospital, has shown that a team approach is required to offer high-quality patient care. This approach also helps to break down professional barriers and mistrust.

Finally, the multiprofessional team, regardless of the specialty or wound aetiology being treated, must recognise that the patient is the central focus for all therapies and treatments.

Education and wound care

Although fragmented, a wide range of educational activities is available for nurses working in or interested in wound healing. At a formal level, programmes are provided through several routes, although only a few universities and educational institutions currently offer them. There is currently no universally-recognised qualification, but a number of programmes are relevant, including some at diploma level in leg ulcers, tissue viability and wound management; other more general programmes also offer modules on wound care e.g., plastic surgery, burns, surgical nursing and acute care; there are also Masters degrees and postgraduate diplomas in wound healing and tissue repair. Emap Healthcare Open Learning offers a diploma-led module in Wound Care, which leads to 20 credits at Level 2.

Outside the UK, nurse specialists are required to achieve at least a degree at Masters level; while this is a growing trend in the UK, it is not yet a requirement. The lack of any formal educational requirement has led to a somewhat patchy uptake of any type of education. A postal survey of tissue viability nurses working in the UK (Flanagan, 1997) reported that only 34% had undertaken formal education in this area and 39% had no academic qualification at all beyond that leading to registration as a nurse. If this relatively new specialty is to be credible, this issue must be addressed and a recognised wound care career pathway developed.

Knowledge, expertise and information can also be gained in other ways:
- By joining associations and societies; these are useful for networking with other interested individuals, and several produce journals and educational packages (Box 12.3)

Box 12.3a Sources of knowledge and expertise: associations and societies

---

European Pressure Ulcer Advisory Panel and **European Tissue Repair Society**
Wound Healing Unit, Department of Dermatology,
The Churchill Hospital, Old Road, Headington, Oxford OX3 7LJ
Tel: +44 (0) 1865 228264
E-mail: OxfordWoundHealingInstitute@compuserve.com

European Wound Management Association
PO Box 864, London SE1 8TT
E-mail: ewma@kcl.ac.uk

Tissue Viability Society
Glanville Centre, Salisbury District Hospital, Salisbury, Wiltshire SP2 8BJ
Tel: +44 (0) 1722 336262 ext 4057
E-mail: tvs.3264@dial.pipex.com

Venous Forum
The Royal Society of Medicine, Membership Department, 1 Wimpole Street, London W1G 0AE
E-mail: membership@roysocmed.ac.uk
Tel: +44 (0) 20 7290 2990

Wound Care Society
PO Box 170, Huntingdon, Cambridgeshire PE18 7PL
Tel: +44 (0) 1480 434401

- By attending conferences and symposia, which will give exposure to the latest research; again, opportunities exist for networking and meeting others interested in the field; these events usually include exhibitions with the chance to see the latest developments in wound management therapies
- By reading a range of specialist journals although mainstream nursing journals also publish articles on a variety of wound management topics (Box 12.3b).

Evaluating effectiveness of care

Nurses, like other healthcare professionals, have been encouraged to review their clinical practice, both systematically and critically. A recognised way of doing this is by clinical audit.

Box 12.3b Sources of knowledge and expertise: journals

Advances in Skin and Wound Care
Published by: Springhouse Corporation, 1111 Bethlehem Pike, PO Box 908, Springhouse Pa, 19477, USA

Journal of Tissue Viability
Published by: The Tissue Viability Society, Glanville Centre, Salisbury District Hospital, Salisbury, Wiltshire SP2 8BJ

Journal of Wound Care
Published by: Emap Healthcare Ltd, Greater London House, Hampstead Road, London NW1 7EJ

Ostomy/Wound Management
Published by: Health Management Publications Inc, 950 West Valley Road, Suite 2800, Wayne Pa, 19087, USA

Primary Intention
Published by: Ink Press International, PO Box 1280, 242 Rokeby Road, Subiaco 6008, Western Australia

Wound Care Society Journal
published in *Nursing Times* by: Emap Healthcare Ltd, Greater London House, Hampstead Road, London NW1 7EJ

Wound Repair and Regeneration
Published by: Wound Healing Society, Wound Healing Laboratory, 9 Centre Drive, MSC 0967, Bethesda Md, 20892, USA

Audit and standard setting

The purpose of audit is to maintain and improve standards of care, in line with the Government's aim to improve health (NHSE, 1993); it is supported by the Department of Health (1993). However, it has been suggested that audit is the Government's way of containing and controlling costs (Rodeheaver, 1995).

The audit process systematically reviews practice, although difficulties have been identified in defining, collecting and analysing pertinent clinical outcomes (Mishriki et al., 1993); in this particular audit, the incidence of wound infection was 64.5% greater when diagnosed on clinical impression rather than on pus formation. This emphasises the importance of defining terms and agreeing outcomes. For patients with wounds and wound-related problems, such outcomes can include healing rates, quality of life, patient satisfaction with the service and patient understanding of advice (Morison and Moffatt, 1997). Other possible outcomes could be related to the standards which have been set; these may be waiting times at outpatient clinics, lifting and handling techniques or even undertaking leg ulcer assessments (Elliott et al., 1996).

The audit process in wound care involves a cycle of activities (Figure 12.1) which is a continuous process (Morison and Moffatt, 1997). It can be performed at random or, more usually, linked to standard setting (where achievement of the set standard is measured during the audit).

Standards are professionally-agreed levels of performance (Morison and Moffatt, 1997) characterised by a commonly-agreed goal which should be:
- Desirable
- Achievable
- Observable
- Measurable.

Box 12.4 The audit process (based on Morison and Moffatt, 1997)

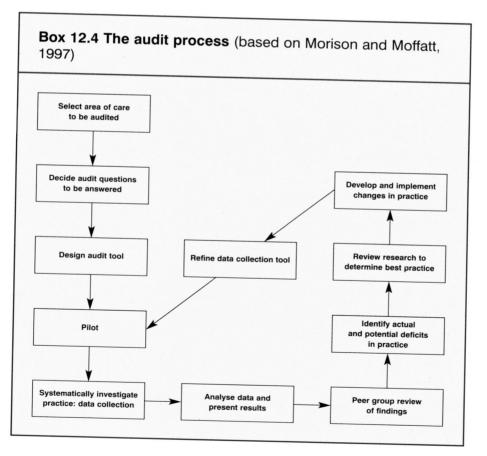

In the USA and recently throughout Europe, a series of standards has been set for the prevention and treatment of pressure ulcers (EPUAP, 1999); these can be used for audit purposes. In the UK, leg ulcer services have received much attention (Box 12.5); common themes for measuring outcomes include:

- Healing rates
- Rationalisation of dressings and bandages
- Nursing assessments.

Other outcomes include quality of life, perception of pain, patient education, pre-treatment ulcer duration and vascular referral.

Box 12.5 Audits undertaken on UK leg ulcer services

Authors	Audit area	Measured outcome
Stevens et al. (1997)	Hospital and community Leg ulcer clinics	Healing rates Quality of life Vascular referral Nursing assessments Rationalisation of dressings/bandages Pain
Vowden et al. (1997)	Nurse-led hospital-based service	Healing rates Nursing assessments Patient mobility Pre-treatment ulcer duration
Kane et al. (1997)	Leg ulcer resource team in the community	Nursing assessments Pain Patient education Ulcer size
Lambourne (1996)	Community-based leg ulcer services	Healing rates Nursing assessments
Franks (1996) Allen et al. (1993)	Hospital-based leg ulcer clinic	Rationalisation of dressings/ bandages Healing rates Nursing assessments

The audits undertaken yielded both positive and negative results, with a number of deficiencies being identified. However, this is a positive outcome in the audit process, as its main aim is to identify areas of need. Through the audit cycle, these areas can be re-appraised and change implemented, then the service can be re-audited.

Clinical governance

Clinical governance has been defined as corporate accountability for clinical performance (Watkins, 1999). Watkins describes its aim as 'to maintain the highest clinical standards through continuing education and research in a committed environment shared between professional staff and managers, in which multiprofessional team working is encouraged'. Clinical governance is concerned with basing clinical, managerial and educational practice on the best scientific evidence. In the UK, the use of evidence-based practice to achieve clinical excellence has been recommended by the Government in several White Papers (DoH, 1997; 1998). Clinical governance aims to guarantee quality improvements at all levels of service. Trusts are accountable for monitoring the standards and quality of the services they provide, and clinical governance is a mechanism to provide protection for both the public and professionals (McSherry and Haddock, 1999); it is the process by which trusts improve the quality of care and prevent breakdowns in services that have in the past led to poor patient care. The key components of clinical governance include developing policies and guidelines that:

- Provide evidence from clinical risk assessment and research
- Provide quality and practice development
- Carry out clinical audit.

Guidelines and protocols

The use of standard setting and the audit cycle is an excellent way of formalising and evaluating care. Patient outcomes can be further enhanced by the development of clinical guidelines, and to some extent treatment protocols. Guidelines have been defined as formally processed, standardised specifications for care that use the best available scientific evidence together with expert opinion (Leape, 1990). Their purpose is to discourage ritualistic practice, which may lead to ineffective care. Their use is also aimed at helping nurses decide on a range of therapies based on research-based evidence.

Although some similarities exist, there are differences between guidelines and protocols:

- Guidelines are flexible, providing a framework for practice
- Protocols are rigid, and used as a prescriptive method of delivering care; they define practice in absolute terms.

In the area of tissue viability in the USA and in Europe, clinical practice guidelines are available for clinicians, patients and carers for the prediction and prevention of pressure ulcers (NPUAP, 1992; EPUAP, 1999; RCN, 2000).

The future

For those with an active interest in wound management these are exciting times. Tremendous advances are being made in a range of areas from dressing materials to equipment and therapeutic devices, together with a structure for delivering effective care. Research is extending the boundaries of scientific knowledge, and the multiprofessional approach brings different disciplines together, helping to break down boundaries and reduce professional jealousies.

Nurse specialists in wound care may be able to follow the example of other nursing specialties in developing their field of expertise, such as establishing a formal group and network with an agreed level of education and qualifications. Clinical nurse specialists working in wound management are in an ideal position to improve patient care. Using their energy, enthusiasm and abilities they have the opportunity to bring other members of the healthcare team together to work as a truly multidisciplinary way.

Whilst the development of the nurse specialist in wound care is an important component of future developments, many opportunities also exist for other nurses with an active interest in the specialty. The societies and networking opportunities should continue to expand and be freely available to all nurses who manage patients with wound-related problems. Hopefully the future heralds a high standard of wound care for all patients, regardless of where and by whom they are treated.

References

Allen, M., Hourston, R., Shoney, B. et al. (1993) Two-year audit of a nursed-supervised leg ulcer clinic in a district general hospital. *Journal of Wound Care* 2: 5; 289–292.

Bale, S. (1995) The role of the clinical nurse specialist within the healthcare team. *Journal of Wound Care* 4: 2, 86–87.

Bale, S., Jones, V. (1997) *Wound Care Nursing: A patient-centred approach*. Hong Kong: Balliere Tindall.

Blair, S.D., Wright, D.D., Backhouse, C.M. et al. (1988) Sustained compression and healing of chronic ulcers. *British Medical Journal* 297: 1159–1161.

Browning, D. (1997) A team approach to pressure relief for people with diabetes. *Journal of Wound Care* 6: 6, 298–300.

Buchbinder, D., Melick, C.F., Hilton, M.M., Huber, G.J. (1997) Building a wound care healing team. In: Krasner, D., Kane, D. (eds). *Chronic Wound Care* (2nd edn). Wayne, Pa: Health Management Publications.

Castledine, G. (1992) The advanced practitioner. *Nursing* 5: 7, 14–15.

Connor, H. (1994) Prevention of diabetic foot problems: Identification and the team approach. In: Boulton, A.J.M., Connor, H., Cavanagh, P.R. (eds) *The Foot in Diabetes* (2nd edn). London: John Wiley and Sons Ltd.

Department of Health. (1993) *Clinical Audit*. London: HMSO.

Department of Health (1997) *The New NHS: Modern, Dependable*. London: HMSO.

Department of Health (1998) *A First Class Service: Quality in the new NHS*. London: HMSO.

Department of Health (2000) *The NHS Plan: A plan for investment, a plan for reform*. London: The Stationery Office.

Edmonds, M.E., Blundell, M.P., Morris, M.E. et al. (1986) Improved survival of the diabetic foot: the role of the specialised foot team. *Quarterly Journal of Medicine* 60: 763–771.

Elder, R., Bullogh, B. (1990) Nurse

practitioners and nurse specialists: Are the roles merging? *Clinical Nurse Specialist* **4**: 2, 78–84.

Elliott, E., Russell, B., Jaffrey, G. (1996) Setting a standard for leg ulcer assessment. *Journal of Wound Care* **5**: 4, 173–175.

European Pressure Ulcer Advisory Panel (1999) *Pressure Ulcer Prevention Guidelines.* Oxford: EPUAP.

Flanagan, M. (1992) The role of the specialist nurse in wound care. *Journal of Wound Care* **1**: 2, 45–46.

Flanagan, M. (1997) A profile of the nurse specialist in tissue viability in the UK. *Journal of Wound Care* **6**: 2, 85–87.

Harding, K.G., Bale, S. (1997) Wound care: Putting theory into practice. In: Krasner, D., Kane, D. (eds) *Chronic Wound Care.* Wayne, Pa: Health Management Publications.

Hollingworth, H. (1993) The specialist nurse in wound management. *Journal of Wound Care* **2**: 2, 114–116.

Humpris, D. (1994) *The Clinical Nurse Specialist: Issues in practice.* London: The Macmillan Press.

Hutton, D.J. (1997) The clinical nurse specialist in tissue viability services. *Journal of Wound Care* **6**: 2; 88–90.

Kane, K., Winfield, S., Prentice, M., Wilson, A. (1997) The leg ulcer resource team: a standard of care. *Journal of Wound Care* **6**: 8; 372–374.

Knowles, E.A., Gem, J., Boulton, A.J.M. (1996) The diabetic foot and the role of a multidisciplinary clinic. *Journal of Wound Care* **5**: 10, 452–454.

Lambourne, L.A., Moffatt, C.J., Jones, A.C. et al. (1996) Clinical audit and effective change in leg ulcer services. *Journal of Wound Care* **5**: 8, 348–351.

Leape, L. (1990) Practice guidelines: An overview. *Quality Review Bulletin* **16**: 42–49.

McSherry, R., Haddock, J. (1999) Evidence-based healthcare: Its place within clinical governance. *British Journal of Nursing* **8**: 2, 113–117.

Middleton, A., Webb, F., Bayliss, B. et al. (1997) Implementation of a pilot project to provide a district-wide mechanism for effective communication in the management of diabetic foot ulceration. *Practical Diabetes International* **14**: 1.

Mishriki, S.F., Law, M.B., Jeffery, M.B. (1993) Surgical audit: Variations in wound infection rates according to definition. *Journal of Wound Care* **2**: 5, 286–288.

Morison, M., Moffatt, C. (1997) Quality assurance. In: Morison, M., Moffatt, C., Bridel-Nixon, J., Bale, S. (eds) *A Colour Guide to the Nursing Management of Chronic Wounds.* London: Mosby.

NHS Executive (1993) *The A–Z of Quality.* London: Department of Health.

O'Flynn, L. (1997) A new protocol to co-ordinate a multidisciplinary team. *Journal of Wound Care* **6**: 3, 109–112.

Panel for the Prediction and Prevention of Pressure Ulcers in Adults (1992) *Pressure Ulcers in Adults: Prediction and prevention.* Clinical Practice Guideline, number 3. *AHCPR Publication no. 92-0047.* Rockville Pa: Agency for Health Care Policy and Research, Public Health Service. Department of Health and Human Resources.

Rodeheaver, G.T. (1995) The US model for national standards of care. *Journal of Wound Care* **4**: 5; 238–239.

Royal College of Nursing (2000) *Pressure Ulcer Risk Assessment and Prevention: Clinical practice guidelines.* London: RCN.

Sibbald, R.G., Kensholme, A., Carter, L. (1996) Specialised foot clinics for patients with diabetes. *Journal of Wound Care* **5**: 5, 238–241.

Stevens, J., Franks, P.J., Harrington, M. (1997) A community/hospital leg ulcer service. *Journal of Wound Care* **6**: 2, 62–68.

Storr, G. (1988) The clinical nurse specialist: From the outside looking in. *Journal of Advanced Nursing* **13**: 266–272.

Sutherland, M.A. (1997) A team approach to wound care in pyoderma gangrenosum. *Journal of Wound Care* **6**: 4, 161–164.

Vowden, K.R., Barker, A., Vowden, M.D. (1997) Leg ulcer management in a nurse-led hospital-based clinic. *Journal of Wound Care* **6**: 5, 233–236.

Wallace, M. and Gough, P. (1995). The UKCC's criteria for specialist and advanced nursing practice. *British Journal of Nursing* **4**: 16, 939–944.

Wright, S. (1991) The nurse as a consultant. *Nursing Standard* **5**: 20, 31–34.

Index